LET US - LET ME

(SEEK: SPIRITUAL MATURITY)

BOOK COVER

The Lord expects us to believe His Words (John 14:1-3) about His preparing a special place for His followers. This is what we should anticipate as we live within His "Let Us" guidelines for our lives. The result and benefit includes:

PSALM 23:1, 3, 5 (NIV)

The Lord is my Shepherd…He refreshes my soul…He prepares His table for me…

REVELATION 12:9 (NIV)

Then the angel said to me: Write this: Blessed are those who are invited to the wedding supper of the Lamb! And he added: These are the true words of God.

THE WORD FROM HIM FOR YOU

MATTHEW 24:44 (NIV)

So you also must be ready, because the Son of Man will come at an hour when you do not expect him.

Are You Ready To Take Your Place At His Banquet Table?

Let Us - Let Me
(Seek: Spiritual Maturity)

James Perry

Let Us - Let Me (Seek: Spiritual Maturity)

Copyright © 2020 by James Perry

All rights reserved. No part of this book may be reproduced or transmitted in any form or by any means without written permission of the author.

ISBN 9781733454018

Dedication

One's life is influenced by different acquaintances and friends/ There is no one that can compare to the special person that has had the best relationship, greatest influence and impact in my life and ministry like my precious wife - -

Peggy Ann Fry Perry

She has maintained a strong faith in the God Who never fails. Amid the pleasant and difficult moments in ministry; the relocation to various geographical locations; training and helping our four children with their Catechism and Scripture memory work – as well as the other obligations of a mother, wife and woman – she has been stalwart and unwavering in her love and encouragement – with her husband and children and in ministry matters.

Even with the writing of a Book, she has spent time reading the manuscripts - making suggestions and recommendations – and she has done so with grace and encouragement.

Proverbs 31:10-12 (AMP)
An excellent woman [one who is spiritual, capable, intelligent, virtuous]...Her value is more precious than jewels and her worth is far above rubies or pearls. The heart of her husband trusts in her [with secure confidence], He will have no lack of gain. She comforts, encourages, and does him only good and not evil all the days of her life.

Foreword

During the winter of 1776-1777 Thomas Paine wrote in his pamphlet *The American Crisis* his famous words: "These are the times that try men's souls: The summer soldier and the sunshine patriot will, in this crisis, shrink from the service of his country; but he that stands it NOW deserves the love and thanks of man and woman." He reminded his countrymen that "the harder the conflict, the more glorious the triumph." He wrote these words to bolster the troops – In August of 1776 General Washington had 28,000 men – by December he had 3,000 because many had deserted and gone home. Life was "easier" under the thumb of British rule – freedom and liberty were costing too much.

An adage says history repeats itself and so it seems within the ranks of those who profess Christ. We who are called to be the light in darkness are fleeing from the spotlight because it is easier to live within our culture. Pastors and leadership have deserted the cause because of their lust for someone who is not their spouse and vocally declared they were wrong in their defense of the faith. So called Christians have rallied with those within the culture who proclaim that one can be with whomever they love when God has specifically forbidden same sex relationships. Transgenderism and gender dysphoria is accepted even though our faith proclaims we were fearfully and wonderfully formed within our mother's womb by God. Holy Matrimony has been diluted as often couples have lived together for years with the reasoning that they want to make sure they are compatible or because they want to save money for the big wedding party. We kill our children while they are still in the womb because they come at an inopportune time, they are an economic burden or they just aren't wanted even though they are a gift from God.

With the rise of the preeminence of the secular culture, today's Christians are facing a backlash that has been rare within our country. While the culture demands inclusivity and safe spaces, Christians have been culled out as the acceptable people to be mocked and derided. Social media bans and deletes Christian groups and their posts that present the truth as opposed to the politically correct thought of the day. Christian organizations are blocked from caring for children and orphans unless they accept LGBT "theology." Christians are sued for their beliefs; they are losing their businesses, jobs and scholarships. In countries outside of the United States our brethren are imprisoned and executed as they minister to others. But this is nothing new – we read in Hebrews 11 that our Christian forefathers and mothers "faced jeers and flogging and even chains and imprisonment. They were put to death by stoning; they were sawed in two; they were killed by the sword. They went about in sheepskins and goatskins, destitute, persecuted and mistreated – the world was not worthy of them. They wandered in deserts and mountains, living in caves and in holes in the ground" (verses 36-38).

Professing Christians are deserting the cause because of a little societal pushback. How did Christians before us endure their persecution? Who will remind us of our calling to "let our light shine before others, that they may see our good deeds and glorify our Father in heaven?" (Matthew 5:16) Who will remind us of the plan that leads to "the crown of life that the Lord has promised to those who love him" (James 1:12)? Who will write to a bolster the troops? James Perry steps up to the challenge in his latest book "LET US – LET ME." We learn that there many uses of the phrase "LET US" in scripture and that this is not a suggestion but a directive. We are challenged to become spiritually mature Christians by following these directives so that we may withstand the many challenges that come our way as ambassadors of Christ. But to do so we must prepare ourselves. We must become men and women after God's heart. How do we do this?

Within these pages we find the process. We begin by bowing down and worshiping our God. We pray continuously for strength, guidance and commitment. We find mentors and those who will hold us accountable. We reflect God with enthusiasm. We become examples and encourage one another. We become the salt and light of this current age. We treat all with fairness and justice. We don't grow weary but we keep pressing on and run the race set before us. We read "LET US – LET ME" and remind ourselves of all the tools available to us to become spiritually mature. We soak in the knowledge and become encouraged by those who have gone before us and preserved. We follow the example of those who have lived in secular societies of bygone days and stayed true to the faith. We remember that the harder the conflict, the more glorious the triumph.

James loves hymns and so in keeping with the theme "LET US", I end with words from a hymn by Dan Schutte entitled City of God.

> Awake from your slumber
> Arise from your sleep
> A new day is dawning
> For all those who weep
>
> The people in darkness
> Have seen a great light
> The lord of our longing
> Has conquered the night
>
> LET US build the city of God
> May our tears be turned into dancing
> For the lord our light and our love
> Has turned the night into day.

Introduction

An important phrase, "LET US" is used throughout the Scriptures. While the Creation was taking place, a discussion and decision was made within the Godhead, Genesis 1:26-28 (NLT), "LET US make human beings in our image, to be like us...So God created human beings in his own image. In the image of God he created them; male and female he created them."

When the Lord returns for His own and the culmination of Creation is being revealed, the song of victory will resonate across heaven, "LET US be glad and rejoice, and LET US give honor to him. For the time has come for the wedding feast of the Lamb, and his bride has prepared herself" (Revelation 19:7).

The use of the Hortatory Subjunctive is used frequently in Scripture. What is the Hortatory Subjunctive? It is a statement that urges others to join in to a specific action. Grammatically, it is the same as the first person imperative. It is easily identified because it will always be the first person plural form of the subjunctive mood. The verb form will be near the beginning of a sentence. It is almost always translated "LET US" and is used as a mnemonic device.

In most instances, LET US is not intended as a group suggestion but a directive that must be followed implicitly. In a day when Israel and Judah are unrepentant, the prophet of God appeals to the people with the hortatory subjunctive as part of the appeal:

Come, LET US return to the Lord; for He has torn us, that He may heal us; He has struck us down, and He will bind us up. After two days He will revive us; on the third day He will raise us up, that we may live before Him. LET US know; LET US press on to know the Lord; His going out is sure as the dawn; He will come to us as the showers, as the spring rains that water the earth" (Hosea 6:1-3).

A passage I think of and reflect upon often, Psalm 95:1-7, uses the Hortatory Subjunctive to direct worship of the living God. The words of worship are:
- LET US sing to the Lord;
- LET US make a joyful noise to the rock of our salvation!
- LET US come into his presence with thanksgiving;
- LET US make a joyful noise to him with songs of praise...
- LET US worship and bow down;
- LET US kneel before the Lord, our Maker! For He is our God, and we are the people of His pasture, and the sheep of His hand."

The largest number of the LET US directive is used in the Book of Hebrews. A major part of the following study is from that book with focus on the various applications of that phrase. However, there are other passages that will be noted as well. Attention will be given to Romans 13:12-14 (NIV),

The night is nearly over; the day is almost here. So LET US put aside the deeds of darkness and put on the armor of light. LET US behave decently, as in the daytime, not in carousing and drunkenness, not in sexual immorality and debauchery, not in dissension and jealousy. Rather, clothe yourselves with the Lord Jesus Christ, and do not think about how to gratify the desires of the flesh.

Attention will also be given to Galatians 5:25-26, "Since we live by the Spirit (His enablement), LET US keep in step with the Spirit. LET US not become conceited, provoking and envying each other." An obvious connection will be made with Galatians 6:9-10,

LET US not become weary in doing good, for at the proper time we will reap a harvest if we do not give up. Therefore, as we have opportunity, LET US do good to all people, especially to those who belong to the family of believers.

Reference will also be made to the basic principle stated in First John 4:7, "Beloved, LET US love one another, for love is from God, and whoever loves has been born of God and knows God."

A text that will be recurring is Hebrews 6:1, "LET US move beyond the elementary teachings about Christ and be taken forward to maturity (spiritual growth in the grace and knowledge of the Lord Jesus Christ)."

May the Lord lead each of us into more of His truth and may He richly bless us as we apply His word. LET US be diligent in studying God's Word and communing with our Father in heaven as we pray without ceasing.

Table of Contents

Introduction 11
1. Let Us Worship 1
2. Let Us Pray 5
3. Let Us Bow Down 11
4. Let Us Be Enthusiastic 17
5. Let Us Be Committed 23
6. Let Us Be Accountable 29
7. Let Us Pursue Spiritual Values 33
8. Let Us Be Earnest 37
9. Let Us Be An Example 43
10. Let Us Be An Encourager 47
11. Let Us Be Discerning 53
12. Let Us Be Confident 57
13. Let Us Stir Up Each Another 63
14. Let Us Have A Clean Conscience 67
15. Let Us Have A Steadfast Hope 71
16. Let Us Have A Prepared Heart 75
17. Let Us Prevent A Heart Attack 81
18. Let Us Always Be Ready 85
19. Let Us Be A Well-Defined Picture 91
20. Let Us Always Be Alert 97

21. Let Us Preserve Confidentiality 101
22. Let Us Behave Honorably 105
23. Let Us Honor God... 111
24. Let Us Be Affectionate 115
25. Let Us Be Compliant 121
26. Let Us Be A Do-Gooder 125
27. Let Us Be Non-Discriminatory.................................... 129
28. Let Us Be Appreciative 135
29. Let Us Be Light And Salt 139
30. Let Us Be Recognizable 145
Epilogue 151

1. Let Us Worship

One of the major transitions recorded in Scripture occurs when David was anointed as the King to replace Saul (Second Samuel 5). A major shift in focus occurs with David's commitment to Worship the Lord as the King of all kings and the Lord of all lords. Many of the Psalms attributed to David speak to the need for one to worship and bow down before the Lord (Psalms 93 and Psalms 95 through 101). Hebrews 6:1 tells us: "Let us move beyond the elementary teachings about Christ and be taken forward to (spiritual) maturity." As this verse is incorporated into one's life, one will need a correct understanding and approach in learning to worship the Lord.

One of the powerful passages on true worship is Isaiah's vision of the Lord in heaven (Isaiah 6). What does he see and what does he hear? What will happen to the prophet as he responds to that which he is observing?

- What did Isaiah see? Isaiah wrote: "I saw the Lord sitting upon a throne, high and lifted up; and the train of his robe filled the temple. Above him stood the seraphim. Each had six wings: with two he covered his face, and with two he covered his feet, and with two he flew."
- What did Isaiah hear? Isaiah wrote: "The seraphim called to another and said: Holy, holy, holy is the Lord of hosts; the whole earth is full of his glory!"
- How did the prophet respond to what he saw and heard? Isaiah wrote: "The foundations of the thresholds shook at the voice of him who called, and the house was filled with smoke. I said: Woe is me! For I am lost; for I am a man of unclean lips, and I dwell in the midst of a people of unclean lips; for my eyes have seen the King, the Lord of hosts!"

- What was the personal result and experience? Isaiah wrote (verses 6-7), "Then one of the seraphim flew to me, having in his hand a burning coal that he had taken with tongs from the altar. And he touched my mouth and said: Behold, this has touched your lips; your guilt is taken away, and your sin atoned for."
- What else did the prophet hear? Isaiah wrote (verse 8): "I heard the voice of the Lord saying: Whom shall I send, and who will go for us?"
- How did Isaiah respond to the appeal he had heard? Isaiah wrote (verses 8-9) "Then I said; Here I am! Send me.
- The Lord said: Go...! The remainder of Isaiah 6 records the Lord's assessment of the people to whom Isaiah is sent.

At a different time and setting, when Jesus visited with the woman at the well, she spoke about her traditional form of worship. Jesus quickly related to her the defining quality of legitimate worship. In John 4:23-24, Jesus said: "A time has now come when true worshippers will worship the Father in spirit and in truth, for the Father is seeking such as these to worship Him. God is Spirit and His worshippers must worship Him in spirit and in truth." What does "worship Him in spirit and in truth" mean and entail?

The Psalmist captured the meaning of worship done in spirit and truth as he wrote from his kingly perspective. He conveys how one should reverence, honor and properly worship the one who is The King of all kings. In Psalm 93:1-2 (NASB) David wrote: "The Lord reigns, He is clothed with majesty; The Lord has clothed and girded Himself with strength; Indeed, the world is firmly established, it will not be moved. Your throne is established from of old; You are from everlasting." A Worship Chorus, Majesty, written by Jack Hayford (1980) captures the thrust of Psalm 93.

Majesty! Worship His majesty!Unto Jesus Be all glory, honor and praise…
So exalt, lift up on high The name of Jesus.Magnify, come glorify, Christ Jesus the King…

In the Blog, Desiring God, John Piper wrote about worship and drew the distinction between inner and external expression of worship. He cites Matthew 15:8-9 where Jesus makes that distinction when He said: "This people honor me with their lips but their heart is far from Me; in vain do they worship Me." The MSG paraphrase states Jesus' words very clearly: "You cancel God's command by your rules. Frauds! Isaiah's prophecy of you hit the bull's-eye: These people make a big show of saying the right thing, but their heart isn't in it. They act like they're worshiping me, but they don't mean it. They just use me as a cover for teaching whatever suits their fancy."

This is in keeping with the reiteration of the Law in Deuteronomy 6:13-15, especially as it pertains to His glory. How should one approach the Lord? The Lord declares: "Fear the Lord your God, serve Him only and take your oaths in His name. Do not follow other gods, the gods of the peoples around you; for the Lord your God, who is among you, is a jealous God and His anger will burn against you…" Connected to this is that which the Lord shared through His prophet (Isaiah 42:5-8), "This is what God the Lord says…I, the Lord, have called you for a righteous purpose… I am the Lord; that is My name! I will not give My glory to another or My praise to idols."

During the celebration of Advent, most of the traditional carols (hymns) have a focus on the gift of God, His Son, and the glory and honor that is given to Him as we unite in singing: "O Come, all ye faithful…O come, let us adore Him." Or, "Hark, the Herald Angels Sing; Glory to the newborn King." Other carols echo these same expressions of worship.

The classic work of George Frederic Handel, The Messiah, and the spectacular anthem The Hallelujah Chorus causes all other Christmas Carols and songs to pale in comparison. The contemporary worship refrain that should stir one's heart contains these words:

> Come let us worship the King Jesus the Savior is born. For the Lord is great and greatly to be praised, Through all the earth - Let us worship the King!

2. Let Us Pray

When I was a boy, someone wrote in the front of my Bible: "Prayer and Praises do in pairs; They have Praises who have Prayers." Prayer is said to be: "An offering up of our desires unto God, for things agreeable to His will, in the name of Christ, with confession of our sins, and thankful acknowledgment of his mercies." Some significant elements essential to prayer are found in Psalm 10:16-18, "The Lord is king forever and ever; the nations perish from his land. O Lord, you hear the desire of the afflicted; You will strengthen their heart; You will incline your ear to do justice to the fatherless and the oppressed, so that man who is of the earth may strike terror no more." When worshipping God and coming to Him in prayer, David enjoined and encouraged the people in Psalm 62:8, "Trust in him at all times, O people; pour out your heart before him; God is a refuge for us."

There was a point in the ministry of Jesus when the disciples came to Him with an important request: "Lord, teach us to pray, as John taught his disciples" (Luke 11:1). Without any hesitancy, Jesus responded (Luke 11:2-5): "When you pray, say: Father, hallowed be Your name..." In a parable Jesus shared with His disciples (Luke 18:1), He asserted: "They should always pray and not give up." In the model prayer Jesus also shared with His disciples (Matthew 6), He indicates the focus that is needed/required when one prays.

- First is reverencing God at the outset of one's prayer. The immediate focus is threefold:

(1) Your name – hallowed;
(2) Your Kingdom – come;
(3) Your Will – be done – on earth as it is in heaven.

This addresses one's identification with God, His purposes and living out that identification on earth in the same way that it is carried out in heaven.
- Second is consideration of perceived personal needs. Again, it is threefold:

(1) Our daily bread – give us;
(2) Forgive - us as we have forgiven others;
(3) Lead us/Deliver us – from temptations and evil.

The Bible is replete with other examples of ways one can pray:

- Prayer of Thanksgiving (Psalms 100): Enter into His presence with Thanksgiving and Praise.

- Prayer of Supplication (Philippians 4:6-7): By prayer and petition, with thanksgiving, present your requests to God.

- Prayer of Intercession (First Timothy 2:1-2): I urge that petitions, prayers, intercessions, and thanksgiving be offered on behalf of all men for kings and all those in authority.

- Prayer of Imprecation (Psalms 58, 59) to pray in terms of a curse upon those in opposition or to speak evil against them to the Lord. It is being in agreement with that which God will execute.

- Prayer of Worship (Luke 11 and Matthew 6). The prayer of thanksgiving is based upon what God has done. The prayer of worship focuses on who God is – His power, authority, sovereignty.

- Prayer of Consecration (Leviticus 11, Matthew 5:48). It is the recognition that holiness must be a priority because (Hebrews 12:14), I must "be holy; without holiness no one will see the Lord." (Leviticus 11:44), the Lord asserts: 'I am the Lord your God; consecrate yourselves and be holy, because I am holy."

There are other specifics that can be thought of as subjects or categories of prayer. The prayer of faith when one acknowledges the need for forgiveness of sins and a personal

Savior. The prayer for healing and the criteria for offering prayer in this way.

A basic foundation for prayer is given in James 5:13-17 (MSG), "Are you hurting? Pray. Do you feel great? Sing. Are you sick? Call the church leaders together to pray and anoint you with oil in the name of the Master. Believing-prayer will heal you, and Jesus will put you on your feet. And if you've sinned, you'll be forgiven—healed inside and out. Make this your common practice: Confess your sins to each other and pray for each other so that you can live together whole and healed. The prayer of a person living right with God is something powerful to be reckoned with."

One form of prayer that is not used as often as it should be is the prayer of contrition and brokenness. A careful reading of Psalms 31, 32 and 51 illustrate how one deals with personal sin and seeks God's forgiveness and cleansing from that sin. Some of the expressions in Psalms 32 describe David's sense of hopelessness, despair, regret and aloneness. David begins (V. 1), "Blessed is the one whose transgression is forgiven, whose sin is covered." (V. 3-4), "When I kept silent, my bones wasted away through my groaning all day long. For day and night your hand was heavy upon me; my strength was dried up…"

How can David find relief for the anguish of his soul? How can he find restoration within God's favor? What will be required of him to become squared away before God? It is evidenced in Psalms 51 when David cries out for the mercy and grace of God, "Have mercy on me, O God, according to your steadfast love; according to Your abundant mercy, blot out my sins – (adultery and facilitating murder) – (all my) transgressions. Wash me thoroughly from my iniquity, and cleanse me from my sin…Against you, you only, have I sinned and done what is evil in your sight, so that you may be justified in your words and blameless in your judgment."

Psalms 51:10-12 is a prayer of David with which we can readily identify: "Create in me a clean heart, O God, and renew a right spirit within me. Cast me not away from your presence, and take not your Holy Spirit from me. Restore to me the joy of your salvation, and uphold me with a willing spirit." Why can we – should we – readily identify with this prayer? Just a couple of the Biblical reasons: First Corinthians 10:13 (NLT), "The temptations in your life are no different from what others experience. And God is faithful. He will not allow the temptation to be more than you can stand. When you are tempted, he will show you a way out so that you can endure."

First John 1:9-10 reminds us, "If we confess our sins, he is faithful and just to forgive us our sins and to cleanse us from all unrighteousness. If we say we have not sinned, we make Him a liar, and His word is not in us." In James 5:16 (NLT) "Confess your sins to each other and pray for each other so that you may be healed. The earnest prayer of a righteous person has great power and produces wonderful results."

When David wrestled with his sin and how he could avoid confessing it, he was perplexed and miserable. He wanted to avoid confessing his faults and his sins. What brought about the resolve in his life was his understanding of the awfulness of his sin in God's sight. His conclusion is one all of us should remember Psalms 51:16-17, "For You, Lord, will not delight in sacrifice, or I would give it; You will not be pleased with a burnt offering. The sacrifices of God are a broken spirit; a broken and contrite heart, O God, You will not despise." If only, brokenness and contriteness were more easily reached before our Lord.

In 1873, P.P. Bliss wrote a hymn about holiness that included some lines that express where "Let Us – Let Me" must be in our prayers to our Lord.

More holiness give me, more strivings within.
... more sorrow for sin.

More zeal for His glory, more hope in His Word.

More purity give me, more strength to overcome,
More freedom from earth-stains...
More fit for the kingdom, more useful I'd be,
More blessed and holy, more, Savior, like Thee.

3. Let Us Bow Down

It is difficult to appreciate the customs and practices of Royalty. It seems strange that in the presence of a King or Queen women should courtesy and men should bow. We have knowledge of these traditions and customs but are awkward when it comes to employing them. This sense of awkwardness also surfaces when it comes to our understanding of being in the presence of God and our acknowledgement of Him as explained to us in Scripture. A popular worship chorus, His Name Is Wonderful, has a line in it that says: "Bow down before Him, Love and adore Him; His name is wonderful, Jesus my Lord." Several obvious questions arise: Do we bow down figuratively or actually? Are we suggesting this is done mentally rather than physically? When we teach this chorus to children, how do we define what the words we have sung mean?

In Psalms 95:6-7, David exudes what should be done in the presence of God: "Oh come, let us worship and bow down; let us kneel before the Lord, our Maker! For He is our God..." Is David speaking as a king of a nation and how he as king should respond to the King of all kings who is in heaven? Is David instructing the nation how they should fear, reverence and honor God, the King? Is David speaking of how people are to appear before him and the expectation of what should take place in his presence as people honor him? Or, is David instructing people that how they react and respond to an earthly king is only a shadow and example for how one is to approach the King of all kings?

There are two New Testament passages that explain how the Biblical Christian is to respond to secular authorities. Romans 13:1-7, "Every person is to be subject to the governing authorities. For there is no authority except from

God, and those that exist have been instituted by God." The passage goes to instruct how one should respond when it comes to laws, taxes and other revenues because the governing authority "is God's servant for your good." The second example is found in First Peter 2:13-17. The tyrant Nero was persecuting Christians when Peter instructed them to: "Be subject for the Lord's sake to every human institution, whether it be to the emperor as supreme, or to governors as sent by him to punish those who do evil and to praise those who do good."

Why should this be the behavior and action of the people? Peter quickly states: For this is the will of God, that by doing good you should put to silence the ignorance of foolish people." The lifestyle of God's people is not to be influenced by the culture or government pressures. He wants the redeemed people to remember how they are to live: "Live as people who are free, not using your freedom as a cover-up for evil, but living as servants of God. Honor everyone… Honor the emperor." The NLT states: "Fear God, and respect the king." The MSG paraphrases verses 13-17, "Make the Master proud of you by being good citizens. Respect the authorities, whatever their level; they are God's emissaries for keeping order. It is God's will that by doing good, you might cure the ignorance of the fools who think you're a danger to society. Exercise your freedom by serving God, not by breaking the rules. Treat everyone you meet with dignity. Love your spiritual family. Revere God. Respect the government."

Should the Biblical Christian bow down to a despotic dictator? Daniel 3 sets the scene of King Nebuchadnezzar and his construction of an image of himself. At specific times during each day, all the people were to bow down and pay homage to his idol. Some of the king's astrologers came to the king and said: "There are some Jews whom you have set over the affairs of the province of Babylon, Shadrach, Meshach and Abednego, who pay no attention to you, Your Majesty. They neither serve your gods nor worship the image of gold you have set up." This caused the king to become furious with rage. The king asks them if they understood what they were supposed to do when hearing the sound of the musical instruments. It was reiterated that if they failed to compromise they would be thrown alive into a blazing furnace.

They gave their unambiguous and uncompromised response: "King Nebuchadnezzar, we do not need to defend ourselves before you in this matter. If we are thrown into the blazing furnace, the God we serve is able to deliver us from it, and He will deliver us from Your Majesty's hand. But even if He does not, we want you to know, Your Majesty, that we will not serve your gods or worship the image of gold you have set up." Despite the furious rage of the king and the intense blaze of the furnace, they persevered and the Lord delivered them unharmed from the fire.

Years passed and Darius was now the king. Daniel 6 tells us that those desiring power under Darius targeted Daniel as an obstruction to their ambitions. They tried to find something – anything – by which Daniel could be discredited but to no avail. Daniel 6:4 states, "The administrators and the satraps tried to find grounds for charges against Daniel in his conduct of government affairs, but they were unable to do so. They could find no corruption in him, because he was trustworthy and neither corrupt nor negligent."

What could they find to discredit this one who early in his captivity (Daniel 1:8) "purposed in his heart that he would not defile himself before God?" The opposition to Daniel was relentless. They finally concluded: "We will never find any basis for charges against this man Daniel unless it has something to do with the law of his God." (Daniel 6:5) What did they determine about Daniel? They watched and realized that he was a man who prayed regularly. The opposition decided this was the basis by which they would eliminate Daniel and his influence in the kingdom. They reported to the king that Daniel was violating the king's edict and that because of his defiance he should be put to death.

Daniel 6:16-18 recounts that "the king gave the order, and they brought Daniel and threw him into the lions' den. The king said to Daniel: May your God, whom you serve continually, rescue you! A stone was brought and placed over the mouth of the den, and the king sealed it with his own signet ring and with the rings of his nobles, so that Daniel's situation might not be changed." The nobles were pleased but the king was distraught. "The king returned to his palace and spent the night without eating and without any entertainment being brought to him. And he could not sleep." Why? His heart was tender toward Daniel and the king respected him. But – he did what the law required him to do. That was that! The deed was done. Daniel had been punished according to the law. What was the rest of the story?

Daniel 6:19-23, "The king got up and hurried to the lions' den. When he came near the den, he called to Daniel in an anguished voice: Daniel, servant of the living God, has your God, whom you serve continually, been able to rescue you from the lions? Daniel answered: May the king live forever! My God sent his angel, and he shut the mouths of the lions. They have not hurt me, because I was found innocent in His sight. Nor have I ever done any wrong before you, Your Majesty. The king was overjoyed and gave orders to lift Daniel out of the den. And when Daniel was lifted from the den, no wound was found on him, because he had trusted in his God."

Daniel and his three companions would not compromise their commitment and loyalty to their King of kings and Lord. They would bow down only to Him and to none other. They would adhere to the guideline of King David who had written Psalms 95:6-7, "To worship and bow down; to kneel before the Lord, their Maker!"

Francis S. Key (1832) wrote the words to the Hymn, Before The Lord We Bow.

> Before the Lord we bow,
> the God who reigns above,
> And rules the world below,
> boundless in power and love.
> Our thanks we bring in joy and praise,
> our hearts we raise
> To Heaven's high King.

May this be the constant song of our heart! It must be a regular part of how we honor and worship "Heaven's high King."

4. Let Us Be Enthusiastic

Is it possible that a secular malaise (uneasiness, purposeless) has infiltrated and impacted the twenty-first century Church? Is there the presence of matter-of-factness where there should be focus and expectation? If so, what do you see as the reason for this shift from the moral high-ground of the Scriptures? Why have professing Christians allowed the church they attend to be more like a Hospice (keeping the patient comfortable until imminent death occurs) and less like a spiritual Hospital whose focus is to reach the lost with the Gospel so they can be made whole in Christ and receive life more abundantly (John 10:10 – ESV)?

One of the things increasingly absent from Church attendees is a cutting-edge enthusiasm for the things of God. One who would not be identified as an "Evangelical Biblical Scholar" – Ralph Waldo Emerson – shared a thought and word that can have a tremendous impact in individual lives as well as on corporate religious gatherings. He spoke about enthusiasm and observed: "Enthusiasm is one of the most powerful engines of success. When you do a thing, do it with all your might. Put your whole soul into it. Stamp it with your own personality. Be active, be energetic, be enthusiastic and faithful, and you will accomplish your objective. Nothing great was ever achieved without enthusiasm." He would later underscore this thought when he wrote: "Nothing great was ever achieved without enthusiasm."

Ecclesiastes 3:9-11 (NIV) shares this perspective of life: "Enjoy life with your wife, whom you love, all the days… God has given you under the sun…Whatever your hand finds to do, do it with all your might, for in the realm of the dead…there is neither working nor planning nor knowledge nor wisdom. I have seen something else under the sun: The race is not to the swift or the battle to the strong, nor does food come to the wise or wealth to the brilliant or favor to the learned..." The force of the Ecclesiastes verses is that wherever one is or whatever one does should be in the commitment and context of "doing it with all your might."

The New Testament counterpart to these words are shared in a cultural context of slavery. Colossians 3:23-24 indicates how and why one should be diligent in labor and work. "Whatever you do, work at it with all your heart, as working for the Lord, not for human masters, since you know that you will receive an inheritance from the Lord as a reward. It is the Lord Christ you are serving." At the very least, one should be enthusiastic in all matters based upon one's relationship with the Lord.

How does this translate to the professing Christian today? Is there a place in one's thinking that "when the going gets tough, the tough get going"? There was a book published years ago that indicated how one should react and think during hard times. The title was, "When You Are Down to Nothing, God Is Up to Something: Discovering Divine Purpose and Provision When Life Hurts." The book promotional was: "Everyone gets down to nothing" at some point in life, whether in relationships, finances, vision and courage for the future, physical or emotional exhaustion, or disappointment with God. Everybody at some time comes to the end of their rope. It's exactly at those points that God does His best work. When we're down to nothing, God is up to something - truths to teach us, answers to satisfy us, assurance to bolster us, resources to supply us, or directions to guide us."

In a series of illustrations about Biblical characters who were down to nothing, one that is mentioned is David. "He was down to nothing. He lost his rights when King Saul branded him an outlaw. He had to flee the country and live among the Philistines. He was a fugitive, at the bottom of the barrel." Despite his status in life due to varying circumstances, what was in David's heart in relationship to the Lord? When the going was tough and rough, what were his thoughts and ultimate actions?

How can one maintain enthusiasm when unexpected and unwanted negatives surface in one's experiences? In the Book of Psalms, there are various illustrations of David's responses and reactions. In Psalm we learn that David was fleeing because of the threat upon his life. As he prays, he expresses the contentment and confidence of his heart (verses 7-8), "You have put more joy in my heart than they have when their grain and wine abound. In peace I will both lie down and sleep; for you alone, O Lord, make me dwell in safety."

A second illustration is found in Psalm 37. David was able to make the distinction between the basis of security of those whose trust is in the Lord, versus the insecurity of the wicked who reject God and His ways. David writes and mentions a phrase "Do Not Fret" three times in verses 1-8, "Do not fret because of evildoers, Be not envious toward wrongdoers…Do not fret because of him who prospers in his way, because of the man who carries out wicked schemes… Do not fret; it leads only to evildoing." He was enthusiastic about the positive alternatives to fretting (being anxious; worrying). His formula:

- Trust in the Lord and do good… cultivate faithfulness.
- Delight in the Lord; and He will give you the desires of your heart.
- Commit your way to the Lord, Trust also in Him, and He will do it.
- Rest in the Lord and
- wait patiently for Him;
- Cease from anger (fretting, anxiety, worry) and
- forsake wrath (or any desire for self-defense or retaliation).

The third Psalm that was significant throughout David's life was the expression in Psalms 122:1, "I was glad when they said to me: LET US go to the house of the Lord!" One commentator suggests: "To go into the house of the Lord signifies to come together where we may have God present with us, as we hear his word; call upon his holy name, and receive help and succor in our necessity." Another commentator suggested: "David was glad when others said to him, "LET US - go." The distance may be great, the weather may be rough, still, "LET US - go."

We should have a similar enthusiasm when it comes to the Lord's House and our regular attendance therein.

Zechariah, in an animated picture of the future glories of the church, described the zeal of the newborn converts: "They cannot but speak of what they have seen and heard, and others must share in their joy. And the inhabitants of one city shall go to another, saying, Let us go speedily to pray before the Lord, and to seek the Lord of hosts: I will go also" (Zechariah 8:21).

In a similar way, when Peter and John were arrested while speaking about Jesus Christ (Acts 4:5-7), "The rulers and elders and scribes gathered together in Jerusalem, with Annas the high priest and Caiaphas and John and Alexander, and all who were of the high-priestly family. And when they had set them in the midst, they inquired: By what power or by what name did you do this?" When they come to their conclusion (verses 18-20): "they called them and charged them not to speak or teach at all in the name of Jesus. But Peter and John answered them: Whether it is right in the sight of God to listen to you rather than to God, you must judge, for we cannot but speak of what we have seen and heard." Peter and John, along with other followers of Jesus Christ were enthused about the power of God and the difference it was making in the lives of those who heard and heeded their message.

How enthused are you about Jesus Christ and His Word? How enthused are you about reaching out to the lost and those in darkness with the message you possess that is light and hope? An old Hymn (1896) written by Palmer Hartsough expresses some of the needed enthusiasm for those who follow and serve Jesus Christ. Such a one will not come alone but bring many others with them to be with Jesus.

> I am resolved no longer to linger,
> Charmed by the world's delight,
> Things that are higher, things that are nobler,
> These have allured my sight.
>
> I will hasten to Him, hasten so glad and free;
> Jesus, greatest, highest, I will come to Thee.

LET US enthusiastically enter into worship, praise, adoration and gratitude to our God and Savior – Jesus Christ.

5. Let Us Be Committed

There is an old saying that if you aim at nothing you will always hit your target. Charlie Brown had a no-fail approach. He would shoot his arrows at the barn and then quickly go and paint the target around his arrows. Sadly, this is the approach of some professing Christians. They have no particular goal but they think they are hitting the bullseye all of the time. While that is positive thinking, it is something else in terms of committed living.

What does Jesus teach about total commitment? He was very clear when He stated to all who chose to follow Him, Luke 9:23-24, "If anyone would come after me, let him deny himself and take up his cross daily and follow me. For whoever would save his life will lose it, but whoever loses his life for my sake will save it." Everyone knew that the cross was a symbol of execution and death. Jesus is teaching His followers that they must die to self every day and live for Him. Paul would later share this call to a life of sacrifice and total commitment in Galatians 2:20, "I have been crucified with Christ. It is no longer I who live, but Christ who lives in me. And the life I now live in the flesh I live by faith in the Son of God, who loved me and gave Himself for me."

Henry F. Lyte (1833) wrote the soul-searching words to the hymn, Jesus, I My Cross Have Taken. Each stanza views the things of life becoming less important or less significant as one's commitment to the Lord increases day by day. He wrote:

Jesus, I my cross have taken,
All to leave and follow Thee.
Destitute, despised, forsaken,
Thou from hence my all shalt be.
Perish, every fond ambition,
All I've sought, and hoped, and known.

> Yet how rich is my condition—
> God and Heaven are still mine own!

Where can one begin to grow in the grace and knowledge of the Lord Jesus Christ? There is no "one" starting place that is superior to another. The point is to start. At the very least, one could start with Psalms 37. Personally, I believe Psalms 37:3-7 (NLT) is the ideal place to begin as there are certain instructions that must be heeded.

- Trust in the Lord and do good.
- Take delight in the Lord, and He will give you your heart's desires.
- Commit everything you do to the Lord. The Psalmist reiterates and underscores: Trust Him, and He will help you.
- Be still in the presence of the Lord. (5) Wait patiently for Him to act.

In the broader context of Psalms 37 we read repeatedly that the committed servant of the Lord should not fret, or be anxious, or worry about what will transpire as life unfolds.

Additionally, we learn in Proverbs 16:3 (NLT), that we are to "Commit our actions (work) to the Lord, and our plans will succeed." The MSG paraphrase is: "Put God in charge of your work, then what you've planned will take place." The AMP Bible indicates: "Commit your works to the Lord [submit and trust them to Him], And your plans will succeed [if you respond to His will and guidance]."

Why is it vital for a professing Christian to be totally committed to the Lord and His Word? In a very terse statement, Hebrews 2:1 warns, "We must pay much closer attention to what we have heard, lest we drift away from it." Several years ago, I heard a dynamic sermon by the late Howard Hendricks on the subject, "The Danger of Drifting" based on this text. The Greek Text for "drift away" indicates the idea of slipping away from a fixed point or the forfeiture of one's faith. The background for the sermon came from research done with 246 men who had been in full-time ministry. As best as he could, Dr. Hendricks concluded that these "pastors" were born-again followers of Jesus Christ. However, within twenty-four months of each other, all had been involved in an adulterous relationship. After interviewing each of these men, Dr. Hendricks compiled four common characteristics of their lives:

- None of the men had any kind of real personal accountability.
- Each of the men had all but ceased having a daily time of personal prayer, Bible reading, and worship.
- More than 80 percent of the men became sexually involved with the other woman after spending significant time with her, often in counseling situations.
- Without exception, each of the 246 had been convinced that this sort of fall "would never happen to me!"

On August 2, 2019 the Baptist Press reported (the following: "Former megachurch pastor Joshua Harris' departure from Christianity has spurred dialogue about apologetics, legalism and the doctrine of salvation. Harris, former pastor of the mega Covenant Life Church in Gaithersburg, Md., announced in July he and his wife Shannon are divorcing, that he no longer considers himself a Christian, and that he regrets having taught that marriage is a union only between a man and a woman." Harris may have said to himself: "This will never happen to me! I love God too much to fall." Sadly, it did happen to him and impacted the lives of his wife and children, countless numbers of colleagues and other followers. It underscores, Hebrews 2:1, "We must pay much closer attention to what we have heard, lest we drift away from it." It also underscores our personal need for total commitment to the Lord and His Word.

There's an old Hymn that shares the warning and danger of allowing oneself to be drifting. Some of the lyrics are: "Drifting carelessly with the tide...Drifting over life's sea." Drifting indicates a lack of direction and purpose. It also indicates the absence of a meaningful goal for one's willingness to just drift. It attaches to the words in Hebrews 2:1, We must pay the most careful attention, therefore, to what we have heard, so that we do not drift away. The additional word of caution in Hebrews 4:1-3 is, "While the promise of entering His rest still stands, let us fear lest any of you should seem to have failed to reach it. For good news came to us just as to them, but the message they heard did not benefit them, because they were not united by faith with those who listened. For we who have believed enter that rest..."

In addition to accountability with one or more in whom one has confidence and where confidentiality will be maintained, another old Hymn, More Holiness Give Me (P.P. Bliss 1873), shares a checklist of areas for self-examination. The basic question: Are there gaps in my spiritual life that need greater attention and increased spiritual growth? The checklist should be used as a much needed personal prayer and should stimulate a much greater commitment to the Lord, His Word, His requirements for His disciples, and His prayer that we be conformed to His image.

- More holiness give me...
- More strivings within...
- More patience...
- More faith...
- More joy...
- More purpose in prayer...
- More gratitude...
- More zeal...
- More meekness...
- More purity...
- More strength...

- More freedom from earth-stains...
- More longings for home.
- More fit for the kingdom...
- More useful...
- More blessed and holy...
- More, Savior, like Thee.

We might want to conclude this self-examination by singing a personal song of commitment...

> To be like Jesus, to be like Jesus!
> My desire - to be like Him!
> All through life's journey from earth to glory,
> My desire - to be like Him.

6. Let Us Be Accountable

Accountability is not always pleasant but it is always necessary. It enables one to remain focused on the existing relationship with Jesus Christ and the life He expects His followers to live. He has made it possible by His life and grace so that each of us can reach His standards – not somehow, but triumphantly. The idea of accountability is suggested in Proverbs 27:17 (ESV), "Iron sharpens iron, and one man sharpens another." (MSG) "You use steel to sharpen steel, and one friend sharpens another." The gist of this verse and idea of accountability is shared in (AMP) "As iron sharpens iron, so one man sharpens [and influences] another [through discussion]."

In the previous chapter that focused on commitment, illustrations were presented regarding the moral compromises different ones had chosen to make as a life choice. This chapter is focusing on what one believes and how easily Biblical beliefs can be compromised. Hebrews 3:12-14 cautions: "Take care, brothers, lest there be in any of you an evil, unbelieving heart, leading you to fall away from the living God..." This may sound as though it is addressing something that never actually happens but the reality is that it can and does happen. Hebrews 3 continues: "Exhort one another every day...that none of you may be hardened by the deceitfulness of sin." The subtlety and reality of sin can and will occur among some of the followers of the Lord. Judas Iscariot is a primary example. In Second Timothy 4:10, Paul speaks of those who have made alternative choices for their lives, such as: "Demas, in love with this present world, has deserted me." And in verses 14-15, Paul states: "Alexander the coppersmith did me great harm; the Lord will repay him according to his deeds. Beware of him yourself, for he strongly opposed our message." In verse 16, Paul goes on to write: "At my first defense no one came to stand by me, but all deserted me." What caused their shift? What had they changed in terms of their belief system? What had they missed in terms of commitment to Jesus Christ and His Word? Hebrews 3:14 best summarizes the primary issue: "For we have come to share in Christ, if indeed we hold our original confidence firm to the end."

The Christian life is not intended to be like a conveyor belt requiring very little effort to attain spiritual maturity and conformity to Jesus Christ. It would be likened more to a treadmill where disciplined steps are being taken so one will be strengthened in faith and practice. After all, we are called to walk by faith and not by sight, aren't we? If the treadmill is turned on and one stops walking step by step, there is an imminent and immediate consequence. If the treadmill is near a wall, one can be banged up against it. One could also fall and begin to get skin burns because of an inability to turn the treadmill off or to regain an upright position. There are safety factors built into the treadmill but they require one employ them, such as the magnetic device pinned to one's garment. In that case, if one fell or lost their grip on the treadmill handles, the magnet would become dislodged and the power cut off. A simple precaution that too many ignore. This is also true in the area of spiritual accountability. If a person can confidentially share with interpersonal transparency, some of the dangers can be avoided and the opportunity for mutual encouragement will be the result. The Bible is replete with the call to persist in one's faith walk. Hebrews 3:6 reminds us: "Christ is faithful over God's house as a son. and we are his house, if indeed we hold fast our confidence and our boasting in our hope." (AMP) "Christ is faithful as a Son over His [Father's] house. And we are His house if we hold fast our confidence and sense of triumph in our hope [in Christ]." This is basic in the interaction of accountability.

I always try to think as comprehensively as possible when I consider the meaning and ramifications of Hebrews 10:24, "Let us consider how we may spur one another on toward love and good deeds." When the text indicates one is to 'consider" an action, it is the end of a positive and strengthening result. The Biblical Christian should comprehend that to "spur" one another has a twofold focus: (1) "to spur" requires a deliberate act to accomplish a particular result. A rider might spur a horse to get it to exert more of its strength so it will go faster or be more responsive. (2) "to spur" had a basic mutual goal and purpose. It is to get love and to show the love of Christ regularly, especially in the area of beneficent good deeds.

The concept of accountability requires a particular mindset and purpose. One is reminded of the words in Hebrews 10:35-36, "Do not throw away your confidence… For you have need of endurance, so that when you have done the will of God you may receive what is promised." Valid accountability will require a change in one's thinking and action. The pedagogical principle is in play here in terms of what one is to know, think and do. Will it be easy? No! Will it require revision of one's mindset and behavior? Yes! As the process unfolds, one is instructed to maintain confidence in the Triune God. Transitions take time but God's grace is always available and is always sufficient. As one endures, there is a reward in one's horizon it is receiving and enjoying all that has been promised.

The primary safeguard for the Biblical Christian and servant of the Lord is abiding in Jesus Christ (John 15). Failure occurs as one slowly relinquishes that relationship and begin to drift away. It will slowly but surely have greater consequences as the drifting increases and one is further and further away from the one in Whom we are all to abide. If we convince ourselves that we would never succumb to heinous sins or that they would never happen to us, we have been deceived. This is the force of Hebrews 3:12-13, "See to it, brothers and sisters, that none of you has a sinful, unbelieving heart that turns away from the living God. But encourage one another daily, as long as it is called 'Today,' so that none of you may be hardened by sin's deceitfulness."

I believe that David was sensitive in this regard. He had known the result and consequences of drifting away from the Lord and His Law. He knew how easily and quickly the deceitfulness of sin could take over his thinking and actions. He eventually reached a point where the things he wanted most were those that would keep him close to the Lord he loved. In Psalms 19:14, he wanted the words of his mouth and the meditation of his heart to always square with God's will and law and to be pleasing in His sight. He would also summarize and pray in Psalms 139:23-24, "Search ME, God, and know MY heart; test ME and know MY anxious thoughts. See if there is any offensive way in ME, and lead ME in the way everlasting." David knew that anyone at any time could drift into heinous sin. From experience (Psalms 32 and 51), he realized the need for brokenness before the Lord. Reconciliation begins with integrity before God; confession of the sin(s) committed; repentance of those sins; and pleading for God's forgiveness. This is one's ultimate accountability. As a reminder, we might want to frequently sing and pray…

All to Jesus, I surrender;
Lord, I give myself to Thee;
Fill me with Thy love and power;
Let Thy blessing fall on me.

I surrender all, I surrender all,
All to Thee, my blessed Savior,
I surrender all.

7. Let Us Pursue Spiritual Values

Throughout one's life there are often inquiries regarding one's goals and ambitions. Recently, a friend posted on Facebook a list of questions that could be asked of students as they began a new school year. Some of them are "fluff" questions but some are applicable in terms of family enrichment and interpersonal relationships. Two of the questions were: (1) What are three awesome things about yourself? (2) What is the one thing you would like us to know about yourself? In family enrichment counseling or sessions, question 2 would add: "that would really make one love you?"

For the Biblical Christian, there are particular spiritual goals one should seek and commitments one must make. When Paul wrote to Timothy about the values he should embrace and pursue throughout his life, he included (First Timothy 6:11), "Pursue righteousness, godliness, faith, love, endurance and gentleness." Paul added in Second Timothy 2:22, "Pursue righteousness, faith, love and peace, along with those who call on the Lord out of a pure heart." Hebrews 12:14 adds, "Pursue peace with everyone, and holiness without which no one will see the Lord." The Message paraphrase is: "Work at getting along with each other (peace) and with God (holiness). Otherwise you'll never get so much as a glimpse of God."

There is intensity with this pursuit and a discipline of life and lifestyle if one is to achieve a desired goal. In the above verses, the summation of the pursuit is one's seeking after godliness (conforming to the laws and wishes of God) and holiness (sanctification: dying to self and living to Christ). It will require total commitment and spiritual maturity to attain this level of godliness and holiness.

What does Jesus teach about total commitment? He was very clear when he stated to all who chose to follow Him, "If anyone would come after me, let him deny himself and take up his cross daily and follow me..." (Luke 9:23-24). It is a learning process as one daily becomes more conformed to the image of Jesus Christ. A contemporary song expresses part of the process:

> Learning to lean, I'm learning to lean on Jesus.
> Finding more power than I've ever dreamed,
> I'm learning to lean on Jesus.
>
> Sad broken hearted, at an altar I knelt
> I found peace that was so serene.
> And all that He asks is a child-like trust
> And a heart that is learning to lean.

When Jesus was informing His disciples that He would soon be leaving them, He did so in the context of preparing them for life without His physical presence in their midst. One of His major concerns was that they learn the necessity of abiding in Him completely (John 15) because within that state there is a special relationship that takes place and certain benefits one can appreciate and enjoy (John 15:7-11). A point that Jesus is making is that His Word, His Love and His Joy will only result from one who is abiding in The Vine. Jesus is very specific in these verses: (Vs. 7) my words abide in you; (Vs. 9) abide in my love; and (Vs. 11) Abide...that My joy may be in you, and that your joy may be full. The Message adds: "If you make yourselves at home with Me and My words are at home in you, you can be sure that whatever you ask will be listened to and acted upon."

John 15 pictures a perfect relationship that is always productive and bountifully fruitful. There is only one thing that can enter the vine that will impact it severely. The damage can occur when a beautiful bird is allowed to enter the vine and slowly build a nest within the lush branches. Before long comes the realization that the beautiful bird is also a carrier of a disruptive and destructive disease. It is known as Phylloxera – a tiny insect (lice) that is not detectible by the eye that will attack the leaves, roots and juices of the grapevine. Jesus may have had Phylloxera in mind when He said that the gardener will have to cut away the affected branches and burn them. This has to be done to prevent the tiny insect (lice) from returning to the vine and affecting more of the branches.

When I attended Bible College, one of the dynamic professors would often state: "Oh young people! You can't prevent a bird from flying over your head – but – you don't have to let it build its nest there." In John 15, we learn how a very small thing can have a great impact and impair the beauty and fruitfulness of the vine. Paul may have had this passage in mind when he wrote in First Corinthians 9:26-27, "I do not run aimlessly...I discipline my body and keep it under control..." He reminded himself and others of the needed care as a branch belonging to The Vine (Philippians 1:20-22), "It is my eager expectation and hope that I will not be at all ashamed, but that with full courage now as always Christ will be honored in my body, whether by life or by death. For to me to live is Christ, and to die is gain. If I am to live in the flesh, that means fruitful labor for me..." Paul's desire, goal and spiritual pursuit was to always be fruitful. However Jesus Christ chose to accomplish that productivity in his life, that's all Paul wanted and sought.

In 1891, Ada Anne F. Whiddington captured the force of Paul's desire and spiritual pursuit when she wrote the Hymn, "Not I, But Christ." The Hymn began and included these words...

> Not I, but Christ, be honored, loved, exalted;
> Not I, but Christ, be seen, be known, be heard;
> Not I, but Christ, in every look and action,
> Not I, but Christ, in every thought and word.

Christ, only Christ! no idle words ever falling,
Christ, only Christ; no needless bustling sound;
Christ, only Christ; no self-important bearing;
Christ, only Christ; no trace of I be found.

8. Let Us Be Earnest

If we are to make any progress at all in giving heed to the "Let Us" passages, one must do so earnestly. There is a helpful example of what must transpire if one is earnestly seeking the Lord, His will and His purpose. David indicated that it was best for him to maintain a focused relationship with the Lord. To that end, he said and prayed, Psalms 63:1-2, "O God, you are my God; earnestly I seek you; my soul thirsts for you; my flesh faints for you, as in a dry and weary land where there is no water. So I have looked upon you in the sanctuary, beholding your power and glory." David saw the need for the totality of who he was to be given over to his spiritual pursuit with the Lord. He knew he must earnestly seek the Lord and be serious in his intention, purpose and effort. He came to the Lord early and often. He came sincerely and zealously. He did not want anything to interrupt or interfere with his commitment.

When various distractions and disruptions occurred, he knew with a certainty that the Lord was his Shepherd (Psalm 23) who would care for and protect him from any adversary or predator. He was confident the Lord would lead him safely through even the valley of the shadow of death. As men and nations struggled to find peace after World War I had ended and the League of Nations was being formed in an effort to maintain peace, Benjamin M. Ramsey (1919) wrote a Hymn – "Teach Me Thy Way, O Lord." Some of the words in that Hymn are helpful for the one facing challenges, distractions, and disruptions that would hinder one's service and ministry for the Lord:

> In hours of loneliness,
> In times of dire distress,
> In failure or success,

Teach me Thy way!

When doubts and fears arise,
Teach me Thy way!
When storms overspread the skies,
Teach me Thy way!

When one sets on a course to faithfully and earnestly live for the Lord and serve Him effectively, the enemy will try to infiltrate that one's life in some way. It may be illness, disability, elimination of a position where one has been serving, or cost modifications. Whatever it is, God is able to deliver us and He will. But even if He chooses not to deliver us, we will not be dissuaded (Daniel 3:17-18).

The words written by Paul, (Ephesians 3:20) encourages one to know and believe that God is able to do immeasurably more than one can ask, or think or imagine. The Amplified Bible expresses the verse: "Now to Him who is able to carry out His purpose and do super-abundantly more than all that we dare ask or think [infinitely beyond our greatest prayers, hopes, or dreams], according to His power that is at work within us."

A faithful friend has re-entered a medical protocol where his explicit trust in God is evident. Cancer is one of the hideous diseases that is relentless in its limitations on one's physical strength and activity. This friend who has been and is an encouragement to me needs to be healed of his cancer that has returned after five years of remission. All of this is very emotional and challenging for me. The friend is Steve Sellers. He is a Barnabas to me and several others. Those whose lives have been touched by him need him and seek the Lord's healing for him. Steve shared the following on Tuesday, August 6, 2019:

I do not know how to thank the Lord for my journey with Cancer. Friend, I do thank Him because of how the Master is using it for His Glory and how He is knocking the rough edges off my life.

One thing I know from my journey is when you are hurting, when the bottom falls out, when future plans are shelved, when you walk into the dark room of unknowns or dreams are shattered, that's when you are brought to a tipping point spiritually. You can choose to blame God and wander in the wilderness of bitterness where you have lost your song. The other choice is to run into your Father's waiting arms, He who is the wellspring of joy even in the midst of one's physical need and suffering.

My choice is to fall into His arms of grace. In my first journey with Cancer in 2013 and now having gone through my second journey it has taught me that when I am desperate He is my source of strength and peace. Prayer is no longer going through the motions, but it's a relational time with my Father. Suffering leads you to the place of surrender where you cry out to the Lord and you learn that He Knows Your Name.

Now, friend, Steve Sellers is still under construction by the Master Builder, so pray for me. I am praying today for those of you who are hurting and feel alone. Praying for those of you battling a disease. Praying for those of you whose dreams have been shattered. Praying for those of you whose marriage is on the rocks. Praying for those who are emotionally wrung out. May you feel the Embrace of the Lord's Grace. May you as Psalm 91 declares: Be at Rest in The Shadow Of The Almighty.

As we think about this dear brother and faithful servant in the Lord, I'm reminded of the words in a Hymn, written by Thomas Moore in 1816 where the mercy of God is being sought...

> Come, ye disconsolate,
> wherever ye languish,
> Come to the mercy seat,

> fervently kneel.
> Here bring your wounded hearts,
> here tell your anguish;
> Earth has no sorrow that Heav'n cannot heal.

The word "fervently" conveys the meaning of one who enthusiastically and passionately is seeking for personal resolve of a need or issue. The word "anguish" expresses the severe mental or physical pain or suffering one is enduring. Coming to the throne of mercy and grace is a place where the sincerity of fervently is known and the anguish of the wounded heart felt.

A verse that is so often quoted (Hebrews 11:6) makes a powerful point for the ones who are earnestly seeking the Lord and His will. (ESV) "And without faith it is impossible to please him, for whoever would draw near to God must believe that He exists and that He rewards those who seek Him." The phrase, "God rewards those who seek Him" expresses the result of one who seeks. The (NLT): "God rewards those who sincerely seek him." The AMP elaborates the dynamic of how God is to be sought: "God rewards those who earnestly and diligently seek Him." The components of the verse are all needed: (1) Faith that pleases God; (2) Drawing near to God; (3) Believing that God exists: (4) God rewards all those who diligently, earnestly seek Him.

A Hymn written by Will L. Thompson in 1880 was a favorite of D. L. Moody and was often sung at the close of an evangelistic service as people were being invited to come to Jesus Christ. The Hymn title is Softly and Tenderly. The words that resonate for me are the appeal of Jesus to the one who has lost his way and needs to find the path that leads to life everlasting. The words are found in the Refrain: "earnestly, tenderly" -

> Come home…You who are weary, come home;
> Earnestly, tenderly, Jesus is calling,
> Calling - - - come home!

As we earnestly walk with the Lord in our spiritual pursuit, the words that should dominate our spiritual being are: "O God, you are my God; earnestly I seek you; my soul thirsts for you; my flesh faints for you…" (Psalm 63:1). Earnestly I seek the Lord. Earnestly I desire to be conformed to His image. Earnestly I purpose to walk by faith and not by sight. Earnestly I seek to know my God and Savior so I can more effectively make Him known.

9. Let Us Be An Example

Jesus made a powerful assignment for His disciples when he told them in John 13:15, "I have given you an example that you should do just as I have done to you." In the MSG, the phrase is paraphrased: "I've laid down a pattern for you. What I've done, you do." There is was to be a behavioral change. That which had always been the duty of a servant, Jesus assumed and indicated that His followers must follow His example. In fact, the disciples were to be an example among all with whom they had contact and to whom they would be privileged to minister. When Jesus spoke of being an example He did so because He wanted His disciples to be examples. What is an example? It is a pattern or model of behavior that should evoke someone to imitate that model. To evoke means to bring or recall within the conscious mind an expected behavior that should always be on display.

Paul wrote to the younger servants of the Lord in a mentoring capacity and in one letter he reminded Timothy, (First Timothy 4:12 - NLT), "Don't let anyone think less of you because you are young. Be an example to all believers in what you say, in the way you live, in your love, your faith, and your purity." Paul is addressing the need for total commitment. He wants Timothy to be successful as he serves the Lord and ministers God's Word.

Paul wrote similarly to Titus about behavior in ministry and that he should purpose to be an example. He also gave the reason for godly behavior, (Titus 2:7-8): "You yourself must be an example to them by doing good works of every kind. Let everything you do reflect the integrity and seriousness of your teaching. Teach the truth so that your teaching can't be criticized." The objective of being an example is that people will listen to God's Word because it is being declared with integrity. It is to be received by the hearers as serious teaching that not only should be heard but also heeded.

To all believers, Paul shared a brief checklist detailing how a believer is to live. He related that it was a commitment he had made for himself. Paul wrote a series of exhortations in his checklist (Philippians 4:4-7). He included the need for the people to rejoice always; to be one who exhibited gentleness; to keep oneself free from being anxious about anything; to be a person of prayer that always included thanksgiving. He added to his checklist desirable behaviors for the people of God. "Finally, brothers, whatever is true, whatever is honorable, whatever is just, whatever is pure, whatever is lovely, whatever is commendable, if there is any excellence, if there is anything worthy of praise, think about these things." (Philippians 4:8). The idea being conveyed is that the child of God should meditate and act upon the things that matter to God because they should also matter to all of His followers.

In verse 9, Paul addresses the example factor when he concluded: "Whatever you have learned or received or heard from me, or seen in me - put it into practice. And the God of peace will be with you." What one had observed in Paul's personal commitment and behavior was to be acted on and deliberately put into practice in a similar way. One commentator suggested that Paul was addressing behavior in all areas of one's life. "Everything that was honest and just toward God and toward people was to be practiced by them, and they were in all things to be examples of the highest kind of morality. They were not to exhibit partial virtues; not to perform one set of duties to the neglect or exclusion of others; not to be faithful in their duties to God, and to neglect their duty to people, not to be punctual in their religious rites, and neglectful of the laws of morality; but they were to do everything that could be regarded as the fair subject of commendation, and that was implied in the highest moral character."

Let Us - Let Me (Seek: Spiritual Maturity)   45

The commentator went on to indicate that: "It is to be remembered that the people of the world, in estimating a person's character, affix much more importance to the virtues of justice and honesty than they do to regularity in observing the ordinances of religion; and therefore if a Christian would make an impression on his fellow-men favorable to religion, it is indispensable that he manifest uncorrupted integrity in his dealings."

James stated very dogmatically that how one interacts in the world, both spiritually and secularly, is measured by the reality of faith on the one hand and practical application of that faith by what it does on the other hand. James wrote it plainly so all who read it would understand precisely what was being required: "What good is it, my brothers and sisters, if someone claims to have faith but has no deeds? Can such faith save them? Suppose a brother or a sister is without clothes and daily food. If one of you says to them: Go in peace; keep warm and well fed, but does nothing about their physical needs, what good is it? In the same way, faith by itself, if it is not accompanied by action, is dead" (James 2:14-17). Anything that is dead is obviously of no consequence and is incapable of responding to anything anymore.

Jesus had established that any one following Him must have compassion on all kinds of people and their varying situations. Jesus wanted His followers to be kind and compassionate. They are to be indiscriminate toward the mercy and grace that is to be shown to others. It is a lifestyle to which one has been called by Jesus. An illustration of what His expectation was is described in Matthew 25:31-46. Jesus is speaking about the final judgment and the criteria which He will use to make the decision. He began by separating the sheep from the goats. Neither were aware of the reason for such a separation except for their being a different species. But it was much more than that. Jesus made the distinction on the basis of how each had behaved in meeting the needs of others and their interpersonal relationships as they did so.

The standard of Jesus is enunciated by Him in verses 34-36. To the sheep, Jesus said:

Come, you who are blessed by my Father; take your inheritance, the kingdom prepared for you since the creation of the world. For I was hungry and you gave me something to eat, I was thirsty and you gave me something to drink, I was a stranger and you invited me in, I needed clothes and you clothed me, I was sick and you looked after me, I was in prison and you came to visit me.

Had they done this to receive special notice or recognition? No! Had they done this to score points with fellow followers or Jesus? No! They did it because of a commitment made to be a disciple of Jesus Christ and to follow His example in the kindness, compassion, mercy and good deeds done. It underscores an important point that what one does is not to receive the notice or approval of other people. What was and is being done was to please Jesus Christ, to emulate who He is, and to bring glory to Him and not to oneself. It was being an example like He had been (John 13:15). The following worship chorus should be the expression of one's heart and life...

> Glory, Glory, Glory to the lamb...
> For He is glorious and worthy to be praised,
> The Lamb upon the throne
> and unto Him we lift our voice in praise -
> The Lamb upon His throne.

10. Let Us Be An Encourager

A reality that is common for all people is their need for encouragement. It may be a positive word or a gentle nudge that assures the other person that you have confidence in them that they will be able to achieve or survive. The writer of Hebrews frames it with a slight difference: "See to it, brothers and sisters, that none of you has a sinful, unbelieving heart that turns away from the living God. But encourage one another daily, as long as it is called: Today, so that none of you may be hardened by sin's deceitfulness" (Hebrews 3:12-13 NIV). These verses open up the spiritual dynamic and the word or nudge for another to keep on looking to Jesus and always have faith and confidence in Him. The ESV uses the word "exhort" rather than encourage to describe what one should be ready, willing and able to do. The NLT paraphrase is: "You must warn each other every day." One commentator suggests the meaning may include:

Intimate friends in the church should exhort, counsel and encourage one another; as or when needed, they should admonish each other of their faults; and should aid one another of the Biblical Christian's requisites."

I like the way the MSG paraphrases these verses: "So watch your step. Make sure there's no evil unbelief lying around that will trip you up and throw you off course, diverting you from the living God. For as long as it's still God's Today, keep each other on your toes so sin doesn't slow down your reflexes. If we can only keep our grip on the sure thing we started out with, we're in this with Christ for the long haul.

If there was a credo that one could embrace, it could be the all-encompassing words in First Thessalonians 5:12-18,

We ask you...to respect those who labor among you and are over you in the Lord and admonish you, and to esteem them very highly in love because of their work. Be at peace among yourselves. And we urge you, brothers, admonish the idle, encourage the fainthearted, help the weak, be patient with them all. See that no one repays anyone evil for evil, but always seek to do good to one another and to everyone. Rejoice always, pray without ceasing, give thanks in all circumstances; for this is the will of God in Christ Jesus for you.

Overall, this would include indiscriminate encouragement of those who are fainthearted and beleaguered. The fainthearted are those who lack courage and are timid. They need to be reminded that God's grace is more than sufficient (Second Corinthians 12:9) and He is able to do immeasurably more than one can ask, think or imagine.

A favorite passage of mine is Judges 8. Gideon has been chosen by the Lord to do a special task for Him. When Gideon recruited an army for the battle (Judges 7), he had 32,000 men. The Lord said to Gideon - there too many men. They might conclude that because of their numbers they would be able to defeat the enemy. The Lord stated that he must tell the men that those who were fearful and trembling needed to return home and leave the battle area. It may have been unexpected but 22,000 returned home and Gideon's army had shrunk by two-thirds leaving him a fighting force of 10,000. The Lord told Gideon that there were still too many. He gave them another test. They went to a brook to get a drink of water. Most of them knelt down and lapped the water. A few scooped the water in their hand and stayed vigilant for any attacking force. Those who lapped like an animal were sent away and Gideon was left with 300 men to face the Midianites.

Just 300 men to fight the assembled armies of the Midianites and Amalekites. Incredible and impossible? The combined armies are described in Judges 7:12, "And the Midianites and the Amalekites and all the children of the east lay along in the valley like grasshoppers for multitude; and their camels were without number, as the sand by the sea side for multitude." The estimate was that they numbered more than 135,000 people. However, Gideon had something that the combined Midianites and Amalekites did not have. He had the encouraging and reassuring word of the Lord that He would deliver them from the hand of the enemy. Gideon did not ask how it would be done. He believed that if the Lord said it, it would be done. What had the Lord said to Gideon? "With the three hundred men...I will save you and give the Midianites into your hands...The three hundred took over the provisions and trumpets of the others "(Judges 7:7-8). "When the three hundred trumpets sounded, the Lord caused the men throughout the camp to turn on each other with their swords. The army fled..." (Judges 7:22).

This was not the end of defeating the enemy. Gideon and his 300 men chased after the confused and defeated army. A verse that we should always remember in our service for the Lord is Judges 8:4. It was observed about the encouraged and reassured group of men, "Gideon and his three hundred men, exhausted yet keeping up the pursuit, came to the Jordan and crossed it." Having been encouraged by the Lord and any shred of disheartenment removed, they kept on keeping on with the enablement of the Lord.

When you are faced with insurmountable challenges and unconquerable obstacles, the questions raised in Psalm 42:5 and 11 should resonate within each one, "Why are you cast down, O my soul, and why are you in turmoil within me? Hope in God..." A similar question is raised in Psalm 43:5, "Why are you cast down, O my soul? And why are you disquieted within me? Hope in God..."

When I enrolled in Columbia Bible College, I had no idea what was ahead. I knew very little about God's will and not very much about God's plan for my life. A passage that was referenced in a Chapel Service captured my heart and mind. The Lord was speaking about a physical battle where the opposition forces were so great and victory was so remote. The passage was Second Chronicles 20:15 where the Lord said:

Listen, King Jehoshaphat and all who live in Judah and Jerusalem! This is what the Lord says to you: Do not be afraid or discouraged because of this vast army. For the battle is not yours, but God's.

Those words made a lasting impact on me from that time forward. It reminds me that we can never remind ourselves too often of the encouraging words of the Lord, "The battle is not yours but God's!" You and I should remind ourselves that the Lord is the same throughout all ages. He gives power to the weak and strength to the weary. His Word is always true and what He says He will do. He is always faithful. He cannot and will not deny Himself.

In 1960, Edith Margaret Clarkson wrote the words of a Hymn based on Second Chronicles 20:15. It emphasizes the fact: The battle is not yours but the Lord's.

The battle is the Lord's!
The harvest fields are white;
how few the reaping hands appear,
their strength how slight!
Yet victory is sure,
we face a vanquished foe;
then forward with the risen Christ
to battle go!

The battle is the Lord's!

Not ours in strength or skill,
but His alone in sovereign grace,
to work His will.
Ours, counting not the cost,
unflinching, to obey;
and in His time His holy arm
shall win the day.

11. Let Us Be Discerning

In one's journey through life, there are always moments when one needs to make primary decisions. It is important to maintain one's priorities and keep a clear perspective so that the decision(s) will be made based upon one's core values and foundational principles. I have always been impressed with the prayer offered by Solomon as he replaced David as king. In First Kings 3:9, Solomon prayed: "Give your servant an understanding mind to govern your people, that I may discern between good and evil, for who is able to govern this your great people?" How will the Lord respond to this request? Will the Lord be pleased with a request for wisdom and discernment? What will Solomon receive from the Lord? Will that exceed his personal expectation?

The response of the Lord (Verses 10-12): "It pleased the Lord that Solomon had asked this. And God said to him: Because you have asked this, and have not asked for yourself long life or riches or the life of your enemies, but have asked for yourself understanding to discern what is right, behold, I now do according to your word. Behold, I give you a wise and discerning mind, so that none like you has been before you and none like you shall arise after you."

The gift of discernment would enhance and increase Solomon's ability to have keenness of insight and judgment; a broadened comprehension. It also included the ability to grasp that which was obscure. If Solomon could rewind his life, this prayer would've come sooner. Why? We read about three good reasons at the beginning of chapter 3: (1) Verse 1: "Solomon made a marriage alliance with Pharaoh king of Egypt." (2) Verse 2: "The people were sacrificing at the high places." And (3) Verse 3: "Solomon sacrificed and made offerings at the high places." These acts were a clear compromise of his core values. Verse 3 begins with: "Solomon loved the Lord, walking in the statutes of David his father." He surely needed "discernment" before he entered into this alliance and compromises.

If only he had known and implemented Psalm 119 as his personal commitment: "Blessed are the undefiled in the way, who walk in the law of the Lord! Blessed are those who keep His testimonies, who seek Him with the whole heart" (Verses 1-2). What would he have gained if this was the way he had ordered his life before the Lord? If only he had applied verses 124-127 to his faith-walk with the Lord: "Deal with Your servant according to Your mercy, and teach me Your statutes. I am Your servant; Give me understanding (discernment), that I may know Your testimonies...I love Your commandments." In the *Treasury of David*, Charles Spurgeon included a possible sermon outline based on Psalms 119:125 regarding the importance of discernment (understanding),

(1) A cheerful acknowledgment: I am thy servant.
(2) A desire implied: to serve more perfectly.
(3) A need recognized: Divine instruction in holy service.
(4) A plea urged: I am Your servant, therefore: Teach me.

Earlier, David had asked a question before the Lord (Psalms 19:12), "Who can discern his errors?" He indicated the perils one can experience in life:

- hidden faults;
- presumptuous sins;
- transgressions;
- words spoken;
- entry of wrong thoughts in one's mind.

Psalm 19:14 is both his plea and claim for deliverance: "Let the words of my mouth and the meditations of my heart be acceptable in your sight, O Lord, my rock and my redeemer."

With a similar concern, Paul prays for the Philippian believers (Philippian 1:9-11):

It is my prayer that your love may abound more and more, with knowledge and all discernment, so that you may approve what is excellent, and so be pure and blameless for the day of Christ, filled with the fruit of righteousness that comes through Jesus Christ, to the glory and praise of God.

Paul is praying that these things will be taken to heart because they will serve as a safeguard against anything that would compromise one's discernment about the Lord and His way for one's life.

There is a need for these words by David and Paul to be a regular part of one's communion and fellowship with the Lord in prayer. We have become so enslaved to set forms and patterns for prayer that we tend to ignore or forget the practicality of "praying without ceasing." We are so apt to begin any prayer with "Dear Heavenly Father" or "O Lord, I need you to guide me...help me in...deliver me from..." Why not be like Peter when he began to walk toward Jesus on the stormy sea. When Peter took his eyes off of Jesus, he began to sink. At that moment, what did Peter think and say? Did he have thoughts that he should've memorized Psalm 23 so he could quote it to Jesus? Did he quickly try to re-construct the model prayer Jesus had taught them in His sermon on the mount? Did he yell to his fellow disciples on the boat to throw him a life preserver? What did he do? What would you have done? Peter said the only thing that expressed his immediate need (Matthew 14:30), "Lord, save me." What kind of response did Peter receive from Jesus? It was twofold: (1) Jesus immediately reached out his hand and took hold of him; (2) He said "O you of little faith, why did you doubt?" (Matthew 14:31) – an important lesson that Peter and the other disciples (including us) needed to hear, learn and remember.

There is another important lesson that should be learned about spiritual maturity in Hebrews 5:12-14:

(1) one should be able to teach the basic oracles of God;

(2) one should be feeding on the solid food of God's revealed Word rather than sipping on milk that children require for their growth and maturity;

(3) solid food is for the mature, for those who have their powers of discernment trained by constant practice to distinguish good from evil"(verse 14).

This same thought is stated in Hebrews 6:1 where the admonition (and rebuke) is, "LET US leave the elementary doctrine of Christ and go on to (spiritual) maturity..." May we know the reality of the powers of discernment that are being trained by constant practice to distinguish good from evil.

> Teach me to love Thee as Thine angels love,
> One holy passion filling all my frame;
> The kindling of the heaven descended Dove,
> My heart an altar, and Thy love the flame.

12. Let Us Be Confident

Spiritual maturity is a lifelong process. The process begins when one confesses with the mouth that Jesus is Lord, and believes in the heart that God raised Jesus from the dead (Romans 10:9-19). It is at that point when the new life in Christ begins and the start of sanctification becomes a reality.. It is "the work of God's free grace, whereby we are renewed in the whole man after the image of God, and are enabled more and more to die unto sin, and live unto righteousness" (Westminster Shorter Catechism 35). Ligonier Ministry adds: "It is a continuing change worked by God in us, freeing us from sinful habits and forming in us Christ like affections, dispositions, and virtues. It does not mean that sin is instantly eradicated, but it is also more than a counteraction, in which sin is restrained or repressed without being progressively destroyed. It is a real transformation." Regeneration is new birth; sanctification is the process of spiritual growth and maturity.

Spiritual confidence indicates the level within one of faith and hope. It speaks with the certainty that promises made by God will be kept beyond what one can anticipate. It is singular in focus. It indicates that one's trust in the Lord is more than adequate to gain the Lord's direction for one's pathway. There is assurance that failure is not an option in the Lord. Paul expressed this in Philippians 1:6, "Being confident (I am sure of this) that He who began a good work in you will bring it to completion at the day of Jesus Christ." What caused Paul to have and share this confidence and certainty? He amplifies this further in Philippians 2:13, "It is God who works in you, both to will and to work for His good pleasure." To be totally clear in his use of the word, Paul expresses in Philippians 3:3 the basis and source of the confidence about which he has written, "We who serve God by his Spirit, who boast in Christ Jesus, and who put no confidence in the flesh."

As an after-thought, Paul mentions that he has credentials that could establish him in the community and be put to fleshly use. He cites them in Philippians3: 4-6,

I myself have reasons for such confidence. If someone else thinks they have reasons to put confidence in the flesh, I have more: circumcised on the eighth day, of the people of Israel, of the tribe of Benjamin, a Hebrew of Hebrews; in regard to the law, a Pharisee; as for zeal, persecuting the church; as for righteousness based on the Law, faultless."

He quickly states that his hope and confidence is in Jesus Christ alone. In Philippians 3:7-8 Paul clearly states:

Whatever were gains to me I now consider loss for the sake of Christ. What is more, I consider everything a loss because of the surpassing worth of knowing Christ Jesus my Lord, for whose sake I have lost all things. I consider them garbage, that I may gain Christ.

He identified himself with the words expressed in the Hymn, Not I, But Christ...

> Christ, only Christ;
> no self-important bearing;
> Christ, only Christ;
> no trace of "I" be found.

This was his song and testimony of confidence in the Lord alone. There would be no compromise and no turning back for Paul. Paul may have thought about the words in Proverbs 25:19 (KJV), "Confidence in an unfaithful man in time of trouble is like a broken tooth, and a foot out of joint." The paraphrase (NLT) wording is: "Putting confidence in an unreliable person in times of trouble is like chewing with a broken tooth or walking on a lame foot." The intent of the verse is obvious. One cannot bite normally nor chew adequately with a broken or loose tooth. In the same way, a person is greatly hobbled with a sprained or dislocated foot. It is even worse if the foot is broken and the bones require a time for healing before it can function once again. The point is that such a person – broken tooth or foot out of joint – fails one when he would be needed most.

A Ligonier Devotional, *Misplaced Confidence*, aims to correct one's focus on relationship and obedience rather than a tribal identity and assumed status. When Jeremiah spoke to the people, he reminded them (Jeremiah 7:3-4) of the priorities that had become blurred. The Devotional says:

Modern people are not the first to read God's Word selectively. Today's passage records Jeremiah's famous sermon against those who trusted in the words 'this is the temple of the Lord.' The threefold repetition of this phrase could indicate the ultimate confidence the people of Judah placed in possessing the temple. Or, it could mean the words formed a mantra the people spoke whenever Jeremiah warned them of divine wrath. Either way, the people of Judah thought God's choice of the nation and His placement of the temple in Jerusalem meant He would never allow the city to fall.

Incorrect interpretation can develop and lead to a misplaced confidence. The people should not have assumed that the Temple was the basis of their spiritual confidence. Their focus should've been on their relationship with the Lord. He was to be their confidence. He wanted them to be a holy and covenant-keeping people. Having adhered to a misplaced confidence, they in fact neglected their special calling to be holy as God is holy.

This same lesson needs to be reviewed by the twenty-first century church. What is the Biblical Church called to be? What are the characteristics and qualities of a people who have been called and have submitted themselves to the Lord. First Peter 2:9-10 states who the Biblical Christian is to be:

"You are a chosen people, a royal priesthood, a holy nation, a people for God's own possession, to proclaim the virtues of Him who called you out of darkness into His marvelous light. Once you were not a people, but now you are the people of God; once you had not received mercy, but now you have received mercy."

The Pulpit Commentary suggests the intention of the phrasing Peter employed in First Peter 2:9.

1. a chosen generation - Peter is drawing a contrast between the disobedient and unbelieving Jews and Christian people whether Jews or Gentiles – Isaiah 43:20.
2. A royal priesthood - Peter follows the Septuagint Version of Exodus 19:6 - the Hebrew states "a kingdom of priests." The word "royal" may mean that God's elect shall sit with Christ on His throne, and reign with him (Revelation 3:21; Revelation 5:10). The royal priesthood is serving Jehovah the King.
3. A holy nation. (Also from Exodus 19:6). The Israelites were a holy nation as separated from the heathen and consecrated to God's service by circumcision. Christians of all nations, and kindreds, and people, and tongues, are one nation under one King, separated to his service, dedicated to him in holy baptism.
4. A peculiar people – (Deuteronomy 7:6) translated by the LXX (Septuagint) a special people. The children of Israel are called the peculiar, private, special, treasured possession of God (Isaiah 43:21). God has now chosen us Christians to be the Israel of God; the Christian Church is His peculiar people, His treasure, a people for His own possession. The literal meaning of the Greek words used by Peter is: "a people for acquisition," or "for keeping safe." Compare with: First Thessalonians 5:9; and Acts 20:28.

In whom is your confidence placed – yourself or The Lord? How well is your life measured by your personal embrace of First Peter 2:9-10? Does this represent your thinking and daily practice in life?

A Poem, (Author Unknown), shares some areas of fears and concerns, versus remembering and discovering the lessons learned about God in one's pursuit of Confidence.

Confidence
When I was young, I feared the dark
With a strong, unreasoned fear.
Yet now the very darkness brings
The knowledge – God is here.

I grumble if a pain is bad,
Yet in my weakest hour
I feel that God is nearer me
With His sustaining power.

I struggle with prevailing sin,
And good things left undone,
Yet find at length, forgiving Love
Is given and not won.

Perhaps the things I grumble at
And do not understand,
Are the very things which lead me
To trust His guiding hand.

13. Let Us Stir Up Each Another

A phrase that deserves our attention and application is: "LET US consider how to stir up one another to love and good works" (Hebrews 10:24). There are more than fifty "one another" references in the New Testament that indicate one's care, concern and involvement with a person or cause. Most of them are focused on one's behavior more than one's attitudes. Twice in John 13:34-35 Jesus states: "A new commandment - love one another. All people will know you are My disciples, if you have love for one another." The writer of Hebrews enjoins the people of God to love one another and to stir up one another to love and good deeds.

"Stir up" and "one another" are connected to each other in Hebrews for a reason. The Word of God is not just for personal consideration as we seek spiritual maturity, it is also intended for interpersonal and relational application. I am to do my part and exert my efforts not just for my personal growth in the grace and knowledge of the Lord Jesus Christ but also for the encouragement of the "one another(s)" who are in my sphere of opportunity.

Years ago while making a choice of paint quality and colors, I came across a useful tool. It was an extended device designed for stirring. The unique factor was that one could use an electric or cordless drill to make use of the stirring device. The shaft was long enough that it could be used in a five gallon bucket of paint. It had one purpose and one purpose only. It was designed to stir from the bottom of the bucket (or can) so there would be unity in the color when the paint was applied to a wall or some other item. But its main purpose was to insure uniformity in color and harmony in appearance.

When it comes to the professing Christian community, "stirring up" has a similar purpose. The goal is to achieve uniformity and harmony. So, the stirring up in the text has as its outcome objective – love and good works (deeds). In Hebrews 3:13, the stirring up will be by way of encouragement. The text reminds us: "Exhort one another every day, as long as it is called today, that none of you may be hardened by the deceitfulness of sin." How often should such an exhortation take place? Answer: "every day." Why is this exhortation significant and purposeful? Answer: "that none of you may be hardened by the deceitfulness of sin." Hebrews 10:25 has the "every day" and "today" statements in view. It conveys a sense of urgency and priority. The days seem to be shorter and the time fleeting. We are to urge "one another" to be guarded so they don't neglect "to meet together, as is the habit of some, but encouraging one another, and all the more as you see the Day drawing near." The "Day" drawing near should always be reflected in how one pursues spiritual maturity and the urgency of the "one another" spiritual care and concern.

Has Jesus indicated anything about the "Day" drawing near? Peter, James, John and Andrew asked Jesus privately about The Day. They said (Mark 13:4) "Tell us, when will these things be, and what will be the sign when all these things are about to be accomplished?" Jesus responds by saying and challenging them (Mark 13:32-33): "But concerning that day or that hour, no one knows, not even the angels in heaven, nor the Son, but only the Father. Be on guard, keep awake (be alert). You do not know when the time will come." The statement is indicating the correct mindset one should have and share with others. The gist of which is, you must be diligent, faithful, and waiting with anticipation for the return of your Lord, who will come at an unexpected hour.

Peter, who was one of the four disciples who raised the question about "The Day", wrote about the impression he received and the certainty in which he believed: "But the day of the Lord will come like a thief. The heavens will disappear with a roar, the elements will be dissolved in the fire, and the earth and its works will not be found. Since everything will be destroyed in this way, what kind of people ought you to be? You ought to conduct yourselves in holiness and godliness" (Second Peter 3:10-11).

Peter is indicating to the scattered and persecuted believers that The Day is real and will happen at some point in human history. It will catch everyone by surprise but the fact and reality is that God's intervention with judgment upon this world will take place. He wants the believers with whom he has ministered to be focused on holiness and godliness in the hostile and relentless world in which they are living. If one lacks holiness, he cannot and will not see God (Hebrews 12:14 NLT), "Work at living in peace with everyone, and work at living a holy life, for those who are not holy will not see the Lord."

Even though Peter was writing to a persecuted church and people, he dutifully reminded them of the Biblical principle and priority for seeking holiness and being holy. It is apparent that despite the ongoing persecution and scattering, he had words similar to Hebrews 12:10 in his mind and heart: "God disciplines us for our good, so that we may share in His holiness." It can be mindboggling to think of the various ways the Lord makes His word, will and discipline known. Try to wrap your mind around and think about persecution being employed as a way and means of God to bring us into a greater knowledge of and sharing in His holiness.

A Hymn that is generally unknown and rarely, if ever sung, was written in 1900 by Lelia N. Morris...

> Called unto holiness,
> Church of our God,
> Purchase of Jesus,
> redeemed by His blood;
> Called from the world

and its idols to flee,
Called from the bondage
of sin to be free.
Refrain:
Holiness unto the Lord
is our watchword and song.
Holiness unto the Lord
as we're marching along.
Sing it, shout it, loud and long,
Holiness unto the Lord,
now and forever.

These words should encourage and grant each of us hope and confidence in our Lord. We should "stir up one another" amid these days of such unrest and uncertainty. Our hope should never be in human government or well-intentioned people. They will and have failed you but Jesus never has and never will fail you.

Jesus never fails;
Heaven and earth may pass away,
but Jesus never fails.

14. Let Us Have A Clean Conscience

The word of God is explicit in its instruction about guarding one's conscience before God. Hebrews 10:22-25 states: "LET US draw near with a true heart in full assurance of faith, with our hearts sprinkled clean from an evil conscience and our bodies washed with pure water." This is the life that one is to pursue and the objective one must gain. As has been written elsewhere, the Hortatory Subjunctive (LET US) is a directive and command for one's behavior. We should personalize the words "LET US" and state them as "LET ME." The text would then read: "LET ME draw near with a true heart and full assurance, with my heart having been cleansed from an evil conscience..."

At some time and in some ways, we all have twinges of conscience regarding one thing or another. It is a good thing that one does because the alternative is extremely dangerous and fatal. Paul wrote about this danger in his letter – First Timothy 4:1-2,

Now the Spirit expressly states that in later times some will abandon the faith to follow deceitful spirits and the teachings of demons, influenced by the hypocrisy of liars whose consciences are seared with a hot iron.

To avoid the seared conscience reality, Paul shared additional instruction (Verses 6-7),

By pointing out these things to the brothers, you will be a good servant of Christ Jesus, nourished by the words of faith and sound instruction that you have followed. But reject irreverent and silly myths. Instead, train yourself for godliness.

Paul makes the point that one must reject the irreverent words that abound and be occupied with training oneself in godliness and how best to live and walk righteously. One must come to grips with the fact that complacency, compromise and procrastination are the tools utilized by our adversary, the devil.

What does it mean to have a heart that is sprinkled clean from and evil consciences and bodies washed with pure water? Several years ago, a testimony by someone connected with the Brooklyn Tabernacle was aired on the 700 Club. Calvin Hunt became a messed up crack cocaine addict and eventually hit rock bottom. He would be out on the streets for days, even weeks, without coming home to his wife and children. He said that he would go to places and do things that he never would've done in his right mind. He became involved with nefarious people armed with weapons. Some of these people were giving up their children sexually to men in exchange for drugs in the crack dens. To Calvin, this lifestyle was becoming more and more like a living hell. When his money would run out, he would find his way back home - pitiful, sorrowful and out of touch with reality. His wife, a woman of prayer and active in the Brooklyn Tabernacle, would always accept him back home. He would find work to do. With the money he earned, he would head straight back to the crack dens. He did this for four years.

One Wednesday after he was away for several days, there was a Midweek Prayer meeting at the Brooklyn Tabernacle. Calvin's wife requested prayer for him. As they were praying – "Lord, deliver and save Calvin." Jim Cymbala, the Pastor interrupted the praying and said: "Here he is." The prayer of the people was being answered in real time as Calvin came walking down the aisle.

Calvin had a beautiful singing voice. In time, he became a member and a soloist in the Brooklyn Tabernacle Choir. Carol Cymbala, a gifted song-writer, composed a song that was a testimony of Calvin Hunt's journey and deliverance from crack cocaine. He would sing the words of the song written for and about him with great emotion and feeling - - -

>There is a blood a cleansing blood
>that flows from Calvary.
>And in this blood,
>there's a saving power,
>For it washes white and makes me clean.
>Chorus:
>I'm clean, I'm clean,
>I've been washed in His blood.
>I'm clean , so clean
>through the power of His love,
>I've been cleansed in the fountain
>of blood shed for me
>oh I'm clean –
>Through the blood of the Lamb – I'm clean.
>
>Only His blood,
>His cleansing blood
>can wash away my sins.
>For I stand today with my heart so clean
>through the blood that Jesus shed,
>I'm truly , truly free
>I'm clean, I'm clean,
>Jesus blood has made me clean.

Can you relate to the words sung by Calvin Hunt? Do you know that your hearts have been sprinkled clean from an evil conscience? Is the testimony and assurance of your life: "I'm clean – Jesus's blood has made me clean?"

John Newton is well-known for the hymns he has written. His testimony is not all that much different from Calvin Hunt's or many other people. At age 82, John Newton said, "My memory is nearly gone, but I remember two things, that I am a great sinner, and that Christ is a great Savior." A biography of his life noted: "No wonder he understood so well grace - the completely undeserved mercy and favor of God." An epitaph on John Newton's tombstone states:

John Newton, Clerk, once an infidel and libertine, a servant of slaves in Africa, was, by the rich mercy of our Lord and Savior Jesus Christ, preserved, restored, pardoned, and appointed to preach the faith he had long labored to destroy.

The conscience is an internal indicator of that which is right and wrong. It is pricked by the Holy Spirit to choose and do the right. Disregard of the Holy Spirit's pricking effectively will "Quench the Spirit" and lead to the searing of the conscience. The searing will be crippling as it becomes incapable of being sensitive to the right and wrong options that confront all of us. The Hortatory Subjunctives in Hebrews 10:23-25 summarize some of the objectives for one's life and walk:

- **Let us** hold fast the confession of our hope without wavering, for He who promised is faithful.
- **Let us** consider how to stir up one another to love and good works,
- **Let us** not neglect to meet together, as is the habit of some,
- **Let us** encourage one another, and all the more as you see the Day drawing near.

<blockquote>
What can wash away my sin?
Nothing but the blood of Jesus;
What can make me whole again?
Nothing but the blood of Jesus.
</blockquote>

15. Let Us Have A Steadfast Hope

What is hope? What is its origin? Where does it get its significance and substantiation? A place to begin is the introductory words of Hebrews 11:1 (NIV), "Faith is the confidence that what we hope for will actually happen; it gives us assurance about things we cannot see." The NLT indicates: "Faith shows the reality of what we hope for; it is the evidence of things we cannot see." When used as a verb, the secular definition of hope is: "To look forward to with desire and reasonable confidence; to believe, desire, or trust."

Two words that stand out in this verse are confidence and assurance. In Hebrews 11 the list of people of faith gives examples of those who were stretched to believe God regardless of events and data that would suggest doing otherwise. These were people who knew God on a personal level. They implicitly and instinctively believed God. In doing so, they established their confidence in God and received assurance from Him. To have confidence means one has trust in another; a trustful relationship exists and prevails. Paul wrote to the believers (Philippians 1:4-7) words that were encouraging to him about them: "I always pray with joy because of your partnership in the gospel from the first day until now, being confident of this, that he who began a good work in you will carry it on to completion until the day of Christ Jesus."

What did Paul mean or imply when he indicated his confidence in the believers? What was the basis and source of this confidence and hope? In Philippians 2:12-13, Paul adds: "My dear friends, as you have always obeyed, not only in my presence, but now much more in my absence, continue to work out your salvation with fear and trembling, for it is God who works in you to will and to act in order to fulfill his good purpose." Paul's confidence is based upon the internal work taking place in the believers as they grow in the grace and knowledge of the Lord Jesus Christ. This is also part of their spiritual maturation process. Paul is confident that this work of God in them will lead to knowing and doing more of God's purpose for them.

Hebrews 11:1 also indicates that faith and confidence gives one assurance about things we cannot see. If it could be seen, it would result in one walking by sight rather than by faith alone. What does assurance mean and necessitate? It means having full confidence in that which God has revealed; it is freedom from doubt; certainty. When confidence and assurance are woven together, it results in one gaining a vibrant and purposeful hope. Romans 5 addresses what is necessary for character building. It also speaks of the triumph of faith in one's life. Verses 3-5 indicate: "We also rejoice in our sufferings, because we know that suffering produces perseverance; perseverance, character; and character, hope. And hope does not disappoint us, because God has poured out His love into our hearts through the Holy Spirit, whom He has given us." The development of Biblical character in the spiritual maturation process results in hope. He noted something special about hope - the presence of the Holy Spirit and God's love in the heart of the believer.

The Holy Spirit in one's heart is not limited to just the presence of God's love. Where the Holy Spirit is present one will also become increasingly aware of His fruitfulness in one's life. Galatians 5:22-23 is just a brief description of how Biblical character and the Holy Spirit are interwoven with each other. The Spirit's presence in one's heart should produce in one's life: "love, joy, peace, patience, kindness, goodness, faithfulness, gentleness, self-control." Ephesians 4:30-32 adds: "Do not grieve the Holy Spirit of God...Be kind and tender-hearted to one another, forgiving each other just as in Christ God forgave you." As these things become more real and evident in one's life, it means that Biblical character and spiritual maturation are taking place. Any wavering in this spiritual growth pattern indicates one is on perilous ground because the Holy Spirit is being grieved.

Hebrews 10:22-23 in the Berean Study Bible (BSB) amplifies the concept of "hope does not disappoint us, because God has poured out His love into our hearts through the Holy Spirit." We are directed: "Let us draw near with a sincere heart in full assurance of faith, having our hearts sprinkled to cleanse us from a guilty conscience and our bodies washed with pure water. Let us hold resolutely to the hope we profess, for He who promised is faithful." It emphasizes that one is to: "hold resolutely to the hope we profess." The MSG renders these words: "So let's do it—full of belief, confident that we're presentable inside and out. Let's keep a firm grip on the promises that keep us going. He always keeps his word." The AMP expresses verse 23: "LET US seize and hold tightly the confession of our hope without wavering, for He who promised is reliable and trustworthy and faithful to His word."

We are instructed to be unwavering; to hold resolutely; to keep a firm grip; to seize and hold tightly. Why these forceful words of instruction? Is there a hidden danger of which we are unaware? We are reminded in Hebrews 4:1-2 (NKJV),

LET US fear lest any of you seem to have come short of it. For indeed the gospel was preached to us as well as to them; but the word which they heard did not profit them, not being mixed with faith in those who heard it.

There is the subtle and crucial blind spot that can beguile one – the Word heard did not profit them because it was not mixed (united) with faith along with those who heard, believed and applied God's Word. When the Word is firmly grasped by those who hear and by faith believe, they will possess an unwavering hope.

In 1891, Fanny Crosby wrote a couple of Hymns about Hope. One of them contains these words:
> Hope on, hope on, O troubled heart;
> If doubts and fears overtake thee,
> Remember this—The Lord hath said,
> He never will forsake thee;
> Then murmur not, still bear thy lot,
> Nor yield to care or sorrow;
> Be sure the clouds that frown today,
> Will break in smiles tomorrow.

16. Let Us Have A Prepared Heart

The aging process is interesting. One experiences the alteration of one's ability to remember details from the past and certain information becomes a blur. There are many things that I recall for which I am grateful. One is the memory of a patient and diligent Sunday School teacher who persevered a class of adolescent boys. He could've done a variety of things but he chose to try and corral us so we would learn more about God's Word and Jesus. One of the things he had us do was to memorize different passages of Scripture (back then, it was KJV). He not only assigned the passage but took time to explain why he thought it was important for us to learn and know. For a period of time, he had us memorize Psalms. That assignment included Psalms 1, 23. 91, 100, and 121.

One passage we had to memorize that impressed and impacted me was Proverbs 4:23. The context of that verse is Proverbs 4:20-23 (NLT):

My child, pay attention to what I say. Listen carefully to my words. Don't lose sight of them. Let them penetrate deep into your heart, for they bring life to those who find them, and healing to their whole body. Guard your heart (keep your heart with all diligence) above all else, for it determines the course of your life.

The phrases that stand out for me are: (a) Let them penetrate deep into your heart, and (b) Guard your heart (keep your heart with all diligence) above all else. Why? "It determines the course of your life." Time and time again, these words have come into my mind and thoughts. In trying circumstances or moments of temptation, I am so thankful for the patient Sunday School teacher who instilled these words and principles into a restless and sometimes disinterested boy.

I understand more now the intention of that patient man and why he wanted us to have the correct focus and to make wise choices in the future. It is so easy to come to the wrong conclusion about people and the choices that they make. One of the most gifted servants of the Lord was the prophet Samuel. After King Saul had disobeyed and acted unwisely, the Lord was displeased and assigned Samuel the task of anointing someone to replace Saul (First Samuel 16). This caused Samuel to be fearful for his life . What if King Saul learned about this action? Would he be put to death for treason? The Lord directed him to do his assignment and he would be divinely protected.

Samuel proceeded to the home of Jesse in Bethlehem (First Samuel 16:6-7) where he expected to anoint a man who would replace Saul as king. When Samuel entered Jesse's home, the first son he saw was Eliab. He took one look at him and thought: "Surely this is the Lord's anointed." Samuel was not correct in his thought. The Lord said to Samuel, "Don't judge by his appearance or height. I have rejected him." What did Samuel have to learn? "The Lord doesn't see things the way you and I see them. People judge by outward appearance, but the Lord looks at the heart." This was and is an ongoing reality. Man looks at the outward appearance whereas God is looking internally at the heart of a man.

Had Samuel come to the wrong home? What lesson was the Lord trying to teach him? The selection process became compounded as one by one Jesse had his seven sons pass before Samuel (First Samuel 16:10). Samuel told Jesse: The Lord has not chosen any of these. Samuel posed one more question to Jesse (Verse 11) "Are all your sons here?" Jesse replied, "there is my youngest son but he's out in a field somewhere keeping sheep." Samuel says: Okay! "Send and get him. We won't sit down until he comes here."

In this moment of suspense, what were Jesse and his sons thinking? What was going on in the mind of Samuel? No one knows how long this delay was or how far away David had taken the sheep. First Samuel 16:12-13, "Jesse sent and brought David in." Being out in the field with sheep, he doubtlessly was dirty and smelly. He may have been weary from watching over the flock throughout the night as he needed to be alert and vigilant to guard and protect the sheep from any predator. He entered his father's house. The text indicates: "Now he was ruddy and had beautiful eyes and was handsome. And the Lord said: Arise, anoint him, for this is he." In obedience to the Lord's direction, "Samuel took the horn of oil and anointed him in the midst of his brothers. And the Spirit of the Lord rushed upon David from that day forward."

Paul and Barnabas recounted this event when they were in Antioch. Luke writes in Acts 13:20-23 (NIV), that Paul addressed the people and gave them a brief history of the Israelites. "They asked for a king, and God gave them Saul the son of Kish, a man of the tribe of Benjamin, for forty years. And when He had removed him, He raised up David to be their king, of whom He testified and said: I have found in David the son of Jesse a man after my heart, who will do all my will. Of this man's offspring God has brought to Israel a Savior, Jesus, as He promised." Take note of the reasons for the Lord's choice of David: (a) He is a man after My heart; (b) He will do all my will (everything I want him to do).

What was in the heart of David, the man after God's own heart, as he walked with and sought the Lord? Psalms 9:1, "I will praise you, O Lord, with all my heart; I will tell of all your wonders." In Psalms 119:34, the commitment of David was: "Give me understanding, and I will keep your law and obey it with all my heart." David was not a perfect man. Would he sin and violate God's Law? Yes! Did he attempt to coverup his transgressions and ignore them? Yes! How could such a man, be a man after God's own heart? What made him different from King Saul?

After his adultery with Bathsheba and his scheme to cover it up, he sunk so low that he gave a command to his General Joab to have Uriah, her husband, killed in battle. After these deeds were completed, David had a restlessness in his soul. Psalms 31:9-10, he began to pray: "Be gracious to me, O Lord, for I am in distress; my eye is wasted from grief; my soul and my body also. For my life is spent with sorrow, and my years with sighing; my strength fails because of my iniquity, and my bones waste away." He progressed to his intense words in Psalms 32:3-5,

For when I kept silent, my bones wasted away through my groaning all day long. For day and night your hand was heavy upon me; my strength was dried up as by the heat of summer. I acknowledged my sin to you, and I did not cover my iniquity; I said: I will confess my transgressions to the Lord, and you forgave the iniquity of my sin.

David had one more major step to take in his sorrow over sin, his contrition and repentance. Psalms 51:1-4, David arrived at his point of confession and the gravity of his sin. This king, a man after God's own heart, had violated God's standards and brought reproach to the name of His Lord. He prayed:

Have mercy on me, O God, according to your steadfast love; according to your abundant mercy blot out my transgressions. Wash me thoroughly from my iniquity, and cleanse me from my sin! For I know my transgressions, and my sin is ever before me. Against you, you only, have I sinned and done what is evil in your sight.

With any contrition, confession and repentance, it is to the end that there will be restoration of one's relationship to the Lord. David has agonized over this and reached the point where he cried out to God, Psalms 51:9-12,

Hide your face from my sins, and blot out all my iniquities. Create in me a clean heart, O God, and renew a right (steadfast) spirit within me. Cast me not away from your presence, and take not your Holy Spirit from me. Restore to me the joy of your salvation, and uphold me with a willing spirit.

Will the Lord answer his prayer? Yes! Will he restore the one who has violated His name and standards? Yes! In 1843, Horatius Bonar wrote:

> I lay my sins on Jesus,
> The spotless Lamb of God;
> He bears them all, and frees us
> From the accursed load;
> I bring my guilt to Jesus,
> To wash my crimson stains
> White in His blood most precious,
> Till not a stain remains.

17. Let Us Prevent A Heart Attack

"The *Medical News Today* reported on the *Ten Leading Causes of Death*. In order, they are:

Heart disease. Cancer. Unintentional injuries. Chronic lower respiratory disease. Stroke and cerebrovascular diseases. Alzheimer's disease. Diabetes. Influenza and pneumonia.

The report on Heart Disease stated:

Many of the top 10 causes of death are preventable through lifestyle changes and regular checkups. Deaths in 2017: 647,457; Percentage of total deaths: 23.5%. Heart disease is the leading cause of death for both men and women. This is the case in the United States and worldwide. More than half of all people who die due to heart disease are men. Medical professionals use the term heart disease to describe several conditions. Many of these conditions relate to the buildup of plaque in the walls of the arteries. As the plaque develops, the arteries narrow. This makes it difficult for blood to flow around the body and increases the risk of heart attack or stroke. It can also give rise to angina, arrhythmias and heart failure. To reduce the risk of dying from heart disease, a person can protect their heart health by adopting a healthful diet and getting regular exercise.

Heart disease and heart attacks are not limited to the physical condition of one's body. There is a spiritual factor that is more real than the physical condition because it deals with eternity rather than just an earthly lifespan. The previous chapter referenced the need to guard one's heart with diligence. The text was Proverbs 4:23, "Guard your heart (keep your heart with all diligence) above all else, for it determines the course of your life."

In the earthly ministry of Jesus Christ, the Pharisees felt threatened by His teaching and actions. They set out to find fault with Him and His followers. Matthew 15:2 (NLT) is one of those occasions when: "The Pharisees ask Jesus: Why do your disciples disobey our age-old tradition? For they ignore our tradition of ceremonial hand washing before they eat." This was the Pharisaical tradition and stipulation they had attached to the Law. What would Jesus do with their objection and criticism? Would He tell His disciples to comply with that tradition? Would it compromise any Biblical standard or set of values?

The focus Jesus wanted His disciples to have was not tradition's ceremonies or physical lifespans. While care for oneself is important, concern about things eternal should never be dismissed or ignored. Jesus first and foremost wanted His followers to have clarity in terms of eternity's values. In Matthew 15:17-19 (NLT), Jesus tells His disciples:

Anything you eat passes through the stomach and then goes into the sewer. But the words you speak come from the heart. That's what defiles you. For from the heart come evil thoughts, murder, adultery, all sexual immorality, theft, lying, and slander. These are what defile you. Eating with unwashed hands will never defile you.

Jesus wanted His disciples to know that the real issues of life would be in the form of a heart attack. Essentially, Jesus made two major points with them about the heart's susceptibility to attack. (a) The words you speak come from the heart so carefully measure what you say. (b) There are things that originate in one's heart that will defile and discredit you. Things such as: "evil thoughts, murder, adultery, all sexual immorality, theft, lying, and slander. These are what defile you."

Those words did not appease the Pharisees and others opposed to Jesus and His ministry. They would continue to oppose Him in any way possible. Despite their best efforts, Jesus would continue to underscore that which His followers needed to know about the heart and its tendency to seek a negative spiritual direction. In Proverbs 23:17-20, are words of wisdom one must embrace: "Don't envy sinners, but always continue to fear the Lord. You will be rewarded for this; your hope will not be disappointed…Keep your heart on the right course…"

One can have mixed emotions when giving thought to the physical heart and the spiritual heart. Physically, if we have an unexpected sensation (pain or numbness), we seek a medical source of assistance. We want the pain to go away and we don't want to die of a heart attack. Anxiety drives us to seek diagnoses, recommendation and relief. Spiritually, we can have sensations caused by a guilty conscience, a sense that something we are about to consider or do is wrong, and we don't want to be caught and held accountable for either the thoughts or acts. Why and how does this happen?

The prophet Jeremiah indicates the Lord's diagnosis of our spiritual symptoms (Jeremiah 17:9-10 NLT). What is taking place within and why is it occurring? The answer: "The human heart is the most deceitful of all things, and desperately wicked. Who really knows how bad it is? But I, the Lord, search all hearts and examine secret motives. I give all people their due rewards, according to what their actions deserve."

The spiritual heart attack should receive immediate attention by the "professing Christian", Why? An answer is given in Isaiah 29:13-14 where the Lord stated: "These people say they are mine. They honor me with their lips, but their hearts are far from me. And their worship of me is nothing but man-made rules learned by rote. Because of this, I will once again astound these hypocrites with amazing wonders. The wisdom of the wise will pass away, and the intelligence of the intelligent will disappear." It dovetails with the words in Jeremiah 7:24, the people "did not obey or incline their ear, but walked in their own counsels and in the stubbornness of their evil heart, and went backward and not forward."

In the early development of the world and the human race, Genesis 6:3-6 (NKJV) indicates: The Lord said:

My Spirit shall not strive with man forever, for he is indeed flesh…the Lord saw that the wickedness of man *was* great in the earth, and that every intent of the thoughts of his heart was only evil continually. The Lord was sorry that He had made man on the earth, and He was grieved in His heart.

With all of these shared truths, how then shall we live?
>With eternity's values in view, Lord
>With eternity's values in view
>May I do each day's work for Jesus?
>With eternity's values in view.

18. Let Us Always Be Ready

If one is ordering his/her life with eternity's values in view, the Hortatory Subjunctives (directives by which one is to comply), are given in Hebrews 12:1-2, 28-19.
- Let us also lay aside every weight, and sin which clings so closely,
- Let us run with endurance the race that is set before us,
- Let us keep on looking to Jesus, the founder and perfecter of our faith,
- Let us be grateful for receiving a kingdom that cannot be shaken,
- Let us offer to God acceptable worship, with reverence and awe, for God is a consuming fire.

Jesus made it clear that one day He would return. The day and time were not the primary focus. The readiness of His followers was (Matthew 24:44): "You must be ready, because the Son of Man will come at an hour you do not expect." What if today we are living in the last days? With chaos, confusion and violence in the world, is it a possibility? If the coming of the Lord is near, what should the Biblical Christian do? How should one live? What should one be? The timely words written by Paul in Romans 15:4-6 (ESV) are significant and helpful:

Whatever was written in former days was written for our instruction, that through endurance and through the encouragement of the Scriptures we might have hope. May the God of endurance and encouragement grant you to live in such harmony with one another, in accord with Christ Jesus, that together you may with one voice glorify the God and Father of our Lord Jesus Christ.

The MSG paraphrase of verse 4: Even if it was written in Scripture long ago, you can be sure it's written for us. God wants the combination of His steady, constant calling and warm, personal counsel in Scripture to come to characterize us, keeping us alert for whatever He will do next.

Is the Biblical Christian ready for what God will do next? What will be happening? Will our spiritual maturity enable us to correctly interpret the times in which we are living? What do we know about the function and activity of the antichrist(s)? First John 4:1-4 states a warning about the antichrists and why the follower of Jesus Christ must be aware and ready. John mentions two immediate concerns for the people of God: (1) The ability to test the spirits, and (2) the real danger of the antichrists. John begins with these words: "Beloved, do not believe every spirit, but test the spirits to see whether they are from God, for many false prophets have gone out into the world." This is as plain and clear as can be. One must be aware of false prophets and the spirits of error. How can one make this determination? John tells us: "Every spirit that confesses that Jesus Christ has come in the flesh is from God, and every spirit that does not confess Jesus is not from God (This is the spirit of the antichrist, which you heard was coming and now is in the world already)." This should be clear and discernible to every spiritually mature follower of Jesus Christ.

Other passages of God's Word speak to the same area and need for one being ready. Second Thessalonians 2:1-4,

Now concerning the coming of our Lord Jesus Christ…Let no one deceive you in any way. For that day will not come, unless the rebellion comes first, and the man of lawlessness is revealed, the son of destruction, who opposes and exalts himself against every so-called god or object of worship, so that he takes his seat in the temple of God, proclaiming himself to be God.

Deception is an attribute of the enemy (John 8:44). What does Jesus teach His followers about the end times and the anti-Christ? Matthew 24:4-27 (NIV) records His explicit warning:

Watch out that no one deceives you. For many will come in My name, claiming: I am the Messiah, and will deceive many. You will hear of wars and rumors of wars, but see to it that you are not alarmed. Such things must happen, but the end is still to come. Nation will rise against nation, and kingdom against kingdom. There will be famines and earthquakes in various places. All these are the beginning of birth pains.

Jesus also shared some issues that will try one's soul (Matthew 24:9-12):

You will be handed over to be persecuted and put to death, and you will be hated by all nations because of me. At that time many will turn away from the faith and will betray and hate each other, and many false prophets will appear and deceive many people. Because of the increase of wickedness, the love of most will grow cold.

With these conditions taking place, what should the Biblical Christian do and be? Jesus indicates the expected behavior of His people (Matthew 24:13-14):

The one who stands firm to the end will be saved. And this gospel of the kingdom will be preached in the whole world as a testimony to all nations, and then the end will come.

Regardless of what is taking place in the world and in the church (so-called), don't allow yourself to be deceived. It is at such a time one needs to discern (Matthew 24:15-21):

So when you see standing in the holy place the abomination that causes desolation, spoken of through the prophet Daniel, let the reader understand, then let those who are in Judea flee to the mountains. Let no one on the housetop go down to take anything out of the house. Let no one in the field go back to get their cloak. How dreadful it will be in those days for pregnant women and nursing mothers! Pray that your flight will not take place in winter or on the Sabbath. For then there will be great distress, unequaled from the beginning of the world until now and never to be equaled again.

Can the Biblical Christian survive the carnage and persecution? While the words of Jesus indicate one will be able to endure, the Biblical Christians will be brought close to the edge of desperation and demise. Jesus goes on to say that times will be difficult and seem to be impossible. He has not forgotten His own, but amid the universal purge, He shares these words (Matthew 23:21-22): "If those days had not been cut short, no one would survive, but for the sake of the elect those days will be shortened." Knowing who you are (one of God's elect) reassures one of the secure place in the hand of the Good Shepherd and His Father (John 10:28-30),

To be able to endure and survive the onslaughts of the antichrist(s), will require both perseverance and wisdom (Matthew 24:23-26),

At that time if anyone says to you: Look, here is the Messiah! or, There he is! do not believe it. For false messiahs and false prophets will appear and perform great signs and wonders to deceive, if possible, even the elect. See, I have told you ahead of time. So if anyone tells you: There he is, out in the wilderness, do not go out; or, here he is, in the inner rooms, do not believe it.

How will the Biblical Christian know when Jesus returns? What should one anticipate? How should one be ready for

Him? Matthew 24:44 specifies: "For as lightning that comes from the east is visible even in the west, so will be the coming of the Son of Man." Are you ready for His coming?

> When He shall come resplendent in His Glory,
> To take His own from out this vale of night,
> O may I know the joy at His appearing,
> Only at morn to walk with Him in white.
>
> When He shall call from earth's remotest corners
> All who have stood triumphant in His might,
> O to be worthy then to stand beside them
> And in that morn to walk with Him in white.
>
> When I shall stand within the court of Heaven
> Where white robed pilgrims pass before my sight,
> Earth's martyred saints and blood-washed overcomers
> These then are they who walk with Him in white.

19. Let Us Be A Well-Defined Picture

If you are like most people, having pictures taken for someone's album is not a favorite moment. To see how others see us can be disconcerting. Our self-image is much different than what is revealed in a snapshot. The older one becomes the sense is, if we had our druthers, we would prefer not to be in a picture that became a permanent possession of another and sometimes posted on the internet. Some people are very photogenic, most people are not.

A snapshot/portrait of a Biblical Christian was on the heart of F.B. Meyer (1847-1929) when he wrote a book on *The Way Into The Holiest.*

Time changes us. Your portrait, taken years ago, when you were in your prime, hangs on the walls of your home. You sometimes sadly contrast it with your present self. Then the eye flashed with fires which have been quenched with many tears. Then the hair was raven and thick, which is now plentifully streaked with the gray symptoms of decay. Then the face was unwrinkled by care, unscarred by conflict; but now how weary and furrowed! The upright form is bent, the step has lost its spring.

He expands his application by writing:

But there is a greater difference between two mental and two physical portraitures. Opinions alter. The radical becomes conservative; temper changes, and affections cool. Names and faces which used to thrill are recalled without emotion. Faded chaplets lie where once flowers of rarest texture yielded their breath in insufficient adoration. Thus is it with those who are born of woman. Time does for them what hardship and authority and suffering would fail to affect. And sometimes the question arises, Can time alter Him whose portrait hangs on the walls of our hearts, painted in undying colors by the hands of the four Evangelists?

The author is quick to remind the reader:
Of course, time takes no effect on God, who is the I AM; eternal and changeless. But Jesus is man as well as God. He has tenses in His being: the yesterday of the past, the to-day of the present, the to-morrow of the future. It is at least a question whether His human nature, keyed to the experiences of man, may not carry with it, even to influence His royal heart, that sensitiveness to the touch of time which is characteristic of our race. But the question tarries only for a second. The moment it utters itself it is drowned by the great outburst of voices which exclaim: He is the same in the meridian day of the present as He was in the yesterday of His earthly life; and He will be the same when to-morrow we shall have left far behind us the shores of time and are voyaging with Him over the tide-less, storm-less depths of the ocean of eternity.

What perspective does the author want the reader to have and maintain? He writes: "If we could ask the blessed dead if they had found Him altered from what they had expected Him to be from the pages of the holy Gospels, they would reiterate the words of the angels - this same Jesus; they would tell us that His hair is white as snow, not with age, but with the light of intense purity; that His face shines still as the sun in His strength, with no sign of weltering; and that His voice is as full as when He summoned Lazarus from the grave, as mellifluous as when it called Mary to recognize Him. Time is foiled in Jesus. He has passed out of its sphere, and is impervious to its spell."

The portrait of the King of kings and Lord of lords. Does that affect the portrait we have of ourselves? Do others see Him in us, or is there so much of us being projected that it blurs who He is and how well one is conformed to His image? As a follower of Jesus Christ who is to be conformed to His image, do others see Jesus in us? As one who is to be under the authority of Jesus Christ and realizing His preeminence in us in everything, is that what our portrait discloses to others? In a strange way, are we living with a photo-shopped representation of what we wish we were rather than a snapshot of who we really are?

Hebrews 13:1-9 lists seven attributes which allows us to determine whether or not we represent who we are and how Jesus Christ sees us. Are these seven snapshots an accurate representation of who we are and how we behave?

Hebrews 13:1-8 - Seven Snapshots:

Vs. 1: Love - Let brotherly love continue. What does this mean and what should it include? Note with: Romans 12:9-10, "Love must be sincere. Hate what is evil; cling to what is good. Be devoted to one another in love. Honor one another above yourselves.

Vs. 2: Hospitality: Do not neglect to show hospitality to strangers, for thereby some have entertained angels unawares. Note with First Peter 4:9-10, "Love one another deeply...Show hospitality to one another without complaining. Also, Romans 12:13, "Share with the saints who are in need. Practice hospitality."

Vs. 3: Compassion: Remember those who are in prison, as though in prison with them, and those who are mistreated, since you also are in the body. The Psalmist describes prisoners and the awfulness of being in chains (Psalm 107:10-14): "Some sat in darkness and in the shadow of death, prisoners in affliction and chains, because they rebelled against the words of God and despised the counsel of the Most High. He humbled their hearts with hard labor; they stumbled, and there was no one to help. Then they cried out to the LORD in their trouble, and He saved them from their distress. He brought them out of darkness and the shadow of death and broke away their chains." It reminded me of the Hymn stanza written by Charles Wesley in 1738 that included the hope of the redeemed...

> Long my imprisoned spirit lay,
> Fast bound in sin and nature's night;
> Thine eye diffused a quickening ray—
> I woke, the dungeon flamed with light;
> My chains fell off, my heart was free,
> I rose, went forth, and followed Thee.

We have that message of redemption and hope for those who are imprisoned. We should make the effort to share it.

Vs. 4: Fidelity: Let marriage be held in honor among all, and let the marriage bed be undefiled, for God will judge the sexually immoral and adulterous. The standard of purity must not be compromised. It is a standard that is to be observed by God's people.

Vs. 5: Contentment: Keep your life free from love of money, and be content with what you have..." The aged preacher was overheard when he mumbled to himself: "It ain't my love of money that's the problem – it's my lack of money."

He had no problem concurring with the remaining words of Paul when he wrote: "...for he (the Lord) has said: I will never leave you nor forsake you. So we can confidently say: The Lord is my helper; I will not fear; what can man do to me? First Timothy 6:6-19 is wise counsel for God's people:

But godliness with contentment is great gain, for we brought nothing into the world, and we cannot take anything out of the world. But if we have food and clothing, with these we will be content. But those who desire to be rich fall into temptation, into a snare, into many senseless and harmful desires that plunge people into ruin and destruction.

Vs. 7: Appreciation: Remember your leaders, those who spoke to you the word of God. Consider the outcome of their way of life, and imitate their faith. Jesus Christ is the same yesterday and today and forever.
Today pastors, church workers, missionaries, Bible college and seminary professors do not always receive words of appreciation for their labors. None of them serve for personal acclamation. That does not mean they should be unaware that they are appreciated. Not enough people consider or contemplate the hardships and challenges that are faced by those who serve the Lord along with their families.

Vs. 9: Awareness: Do not be led away by diverse and strange teachings, for it is good for the heart to be strengthened by grace, not by foods, which have not benefited those devoted to them. It would be good if there were more Berean believers who, having heard the Word, studied, taught and proclaimed the Scriptures to determine whether or not they had heard the truth from the Apostle. Note their action in Acts 17:11-12,
Now the Berean Jews were of more noble character than those in Thessalonica, for they received the message with great eagerness and examined the Scriptures every day to see if what Paul said was true. As a result, many of them believed, as did also a number of prominent Greek women and many Greek men.
In some small measure, may we be like the Berean believers who applied God's truth and saw many others become believers and followers of Jesus Christ.

Sweet is the tender love

Jesus hath shown,
Sweeter far than any love
that mortals have known;
Kind to the erring one,
faithful is He;
He the great example is,
and pattern for me.
Refrain:
Where He leads I'll follow,
Follow all the way.
Where He leads I'll follow,
Follow Jesus every day.
(William A. Ogden – 1885)

20. Let Us Always Be Alert

It is essential for one to be always alert. When I was in Grammar (Elementary) School, I recall one teacher saying when a new assignment was to be made: "Give me your undivided attention." It was always a signal that it would be best for us to listen. In a more technical interpretation, the idea conveyed was that one must be "mentally present and cognitively flexible." This would enable one to think carefully and critically about responsibilities, activities and other tasks.

An article in Psychology Today, June 2011, connects these concepts to multitasking. One of the conclusions drawn expresses:

Contrary to popular belief, human beings cannot multitask. What we are capable of is handling a number of serial tasks in rapid succession, or mixing automatic tasks with those that are not so automatic. That's one of the reasons that the NTSB (National Transportation Board) reports that texting while driving is the functional equivalent of driving with a blood alcohol level three times the legal limit. You just can't effectively attend to two things at once - even the superficially automatic ones.

Another conclusion stated is: "We really can only do one thing at a time, so we ought to do that thing whole-heartedly." Most of our time is spent in the past or the future, rather than the present moment. Someone has suggested, there are two things we can do nothing about. Yesterday because it is gone forever and tomorrow because it is in the future and has not yet arrived. It is impossible to do today anything that will be a final determination for either one. Today is where one is and where one can be constructive in what is done.

For the Biblical Christian, there is one significant mandate that must be implemented each day. The follower of Jesus Christ is directed to: Be Alert. There is a very specific reason for this mandate. In First Peter 5:8-9 (MSG), the Apostle wrote: "Keep a cool head. Stay alert. The Devil is poised to pounce, and would like nothing better than to catch you napping. Keep your guard up. You're not the only ones plunged into these hard times. It's the same with Christians all over the world. So keep a firm grip on the faith." There is the reason and the mandate.

For the blasé and matter-of-fact individual who thinks the devil will never make an inroad into his/her life, Paul was clear when he wrote that no one is exempt from the enemy's pounce. In First Corinthians 10:11-12 (MSG), "These are all warning markers in our history books, written down so that we don't repeat their mistakes. Our positions in the story are parallel—they at the beginning, we at the end—and we are just as capable of messing it up as they were. Don't be so naive and self-confident. You're not exempt. You could fall flat on your face as easily as anyone else. Forget about self-confidence; it's useless. Cultivate God-confidence." The words with which most are familiar from verse 12 are: "Let anyone who thinks that he stands take heed lest he fall."

Any one of us who thinks contrary to these words is headed toward the slippery slope of danger and peril. There is a tendency to think in human terms rather than Biblical and spiritual terms. The historical thinkers remember the unsinkable ship, The Titanic, that on its maiden cruise struck an iceberg. That fabulous ocean liner is now part of a vast debris field at the bottom of the North Atlantic Ocean, 400 hundred miles from the coast of Newfoundland. For many of us, there is recollection of the Japanese bombing of Pearl Harbor in December 1941. The ships and aircraft that had been built to defend the nation were either sunk or sufficiently damaged and made inoperable. Most people will remember for a lifetime the date – September 11, 2001. It was on that day that: "Islamist extremists hijacked four planes that were flying above the United States. Two of them were flown into the twin towers of the World Trade Center in New York. Another was crashed into the Pentagon, the top military building in the capital city, Washington DC. The fourth was commandeered by passengers on the plane who overpowered the terrorists. The plane crashed short of its intended destination."

Why cite these illustrations? The reason is that no one anticipated the sinking of a ship; the destruction of a naval fleet; or airliners being used as weapons to bring about destruction and death. The blasé follower of Jesus Christ can be very naïve regarding the subtlety and ploy of the enemy. There is a sound reason why The Apostle Paul would express that one should "take heed lest he fall" (First Corinthians 10:12). There is a basic and sound reason why The Apostle Paul would emphasize that "The Overseer" "must be well thought of by outsiders, so that he may not fall into disgrace, into a snare (trap) of the devil" (First Timothy 2:7).

The Apostle Peter had similar concerns. To the persecuted believers who were being scattered he said (First Peter 1:13-14 NIV), "With minds that are alert and fully sober, set your hope on the grace to be brought to you when Jesus Christ is revealed at His coming. As obedient children, do not conform to the evil desires you had when you lived in ignorance." The force of his words are clear:

- Have alert minds. Know what you are supposed to believe and wisely make it known. Be aware of the context within which you are living.
- With minds that are fully sober. Don't allow yourself to get caught up with the mundane, superficial or fanciful. Be focused on the Redeemer. (Verse 8), "Though you have not seen him, you love him; and even though you do not see him now, you believe in him and are filled with an inexpressible and glorious joy.

- Set your hope on the coming again of Jesus Christ. Don't let any event or circumstance deny or deprive you from your living hope in a living Savior.

Heed the words of Jesus Christ about His coming again, Mark 13:33-36, "The day or hour no one knows, not even the angels in heaven, nor the Son, but only the Father. Be on guard! Be alert! You do not know when that time will come...Keep watch...What I say to you, I say to everyone: Watch!" In the Hymn, Clothe Yourself With Humility, Susan H. Peterson (1998) wrote:

> Be self-controlled and on alert;
> Satan is prowling round.
> He's like a lion seeking prey;
> Stand firm and don't give ground.

21. Let Us Preserve Confidentiality

Confidentiality with another person is difficult to find. Confidentiality means: "Something spoken or written to one who can be entrusted with secret or private matters." It includes one's confidence in a person that what is shared will remain solely with that person. A person who can keep confidences has always been a rare find. The task of withholding sensitive information has proven even more difficult in today's world of instant access. Wisdom literature shares an observation about confidentiality: "He who goes about as a talebearer (a gossip) reveals secrets, but he who is trustworthy conceals (holds in confidence) a matter" (Proverbs 11:13).

Current trends in politics and media disclosures seem to thrive on "leaking" classified materials that are intended to be kept as secrets. During World War II, it was common to see a poster that used four words to convey why secrets and confidentiality were so vital. The poster read: "Loose Lips Sink Ships." Spreading secrets was dangerous as there were those assigned to work on gaining knowledge of enemy codes to make a determination of strategies for combatting the threat of troop or ship movements.

Proverbs 25:9 contains an important caution for communication with another: "Argue your case with your neighbor, and do not reveal the secret of another," A similar instruction is in Amos 5:13, "Therefore at such a time the prudent person keeps silent, for it is an evil time." The idea is that there will be fewer people with whom and in whom confidentiality is a possibility.

When our son was stationed on a missile base, we walked by one of the missile silos. When I asked my son whether it contained a missile that was armed and ready to be fired, his response was: "I can neither affirm nor deny." I didn't have a need to know. I was just curious as we walked by it. During our visit, a similar military base in the Midwest had been breached. An immediate "Lock Down Order" was transmitted to all the bases. Needless to say, security was high and would be enforced. Confidentiality and Security have a connection. If one casually reveals a pending known strategy for defense or engagement of an enemy, it would advantage the enemy's plans.

A similar incident occurred when we visited a base where our daughter, son-in-law and grandchildren lived. A Terrorist Alert had been issued for the nation. To gain access to the Air Force Base required proper identification and confirmation from an officer on the base. To proceed, one had to slowly maneuver around obstacles and a gunnery outpost. It was not a time for lightheartedness or levity. The country had been attacked (the World Trade Center and the Pentagon). Measures were instantly taken and put into place to prevent any further terrorist attacks against the nation's military installations.

There is an illustration of a suspected breach of confidentiality and security recorded in Second Kings 6. The king of Syria was warring against Israel. Elisha sent word about a pending attack to the king of Israel (Verse 9) "The man of God (Elisha) sent word to the king of Israel, Beware that you do not pass this place, for the Syrians are going down there." The king of Syria was greatly troubled because of this security breach. He wanted to know who violated the confidentiality (Verse 11): "Will you not show me who of us is for the king of Israel?" The fact is that his people were loyal to him and one of his servants dared to state to him (Verse 12): "Elisha, the prophet who is in Israel, tells the king of Israel the words that you speak in your bedroom." The king of Syria dispatches his army and sends them to Dothan to find Elisha. The great army (verse 14) came by night and surrounded the city." The king of Syria failed to factor in the protection of the Lord for His servant Elisha.

Confidentiality is often breached among professing Christian people. One problem is that it is not just a "secret" that is repeated but that the secret has also been embellished by the one entrusted with the information. We have all been with people or sat in a group where during the conversation someone has said: "I probably shouldn't tell you this..." How do you react and respond if or when you hear that statement? Are you curious and desire to know the secret? Or, do you respond by saying: "Please don't tell me about what you were ready to repeat." There is an old saying: "God gave us two ears, and only one mouth for good reason." It is somewhat connected to the instruction in James 1:19 (AMP): "Understand this, my beloved brothers and sisters. Let everyone be quick to hear (be a careful, thoughtful listener), slow to speak (a speaker of carefully chosen words and), slow to anger (patient, reflective, forgiving)." In other words, that which you may have heard confidentially, make certain you do not readily repeat it to anyone else.

Goodreads has several reviews on books about people who guarded confidentiality strictly and sternly. One review is on the 1998 best seller by biographer Ron Chernow entitled: *Titan: The Life Of John D. Rockefeller, Jr.* and how he learned to keep secrets. Rockefeller's Standard Oil Company, in fact, would later become legendary in business circles as an organization where leaking inside information resulted in losing one's job. "You talked...you walked." John D. Rockefeller Sr., for many years the wealthiest man in America, knew better than most the tremendous damage that could be caused by an unbridled tongue.

James 3:3-6 (MSG) addresses the unbridled tongue:

A bit in the mouth of a horse controls the whole horse. A small rudder on a huge ship in the hands of a skilled captain sets a course in the face of the strongest winds. A word out of your mouth may seem of no account, but it can accomplish nearly anything, or destroy it! It only takes a spark to set off a forest fire. A careless or wrongly placed word out of your mouth can do that. By our speech we can ruin the world, turn harmony to chaos, throw mud on a reputation, send the whole world up in smoke and go up in smoke with it, smoke right from the pit of hell.

James then progresses to the tongue of a person. It is small when compared to other functional parts of the body but it has the same potential as a bit in the mouth of the horse, or a ship's rudder controlled by the pilot of the ship, or an ignored spark that can ignite tinder and cause a large forest fire. His point is that the tongue must be controlled. Words that are spoken can have a negative or positive impact. They can edify or destroy reputations.

Paul reminded the people of God in Colossians 4:6 (MSG), "Be gracious in your speech. The goal is to bring out the best in others in a conversation, not put them down, not cut them out." One possible application of Paul's words is: "Just as we should let grace lead whenever we speak, we must also learn to let grace lead at those moments when it would be best to remain silent." Both opportunities require wisdom and discipline. Grace can and should control the secrets we know and enable us to keep them confidential.

22. Let Us Behave Honorably

Meditating on God's Word enables one to glean some useful gems. Hebrews 13:18-25 concludes with a request for prayer, a farewell statement and standard closure. The authorship of the Book has been discussed and disputed since the third century. Some of the discussion by various commentators on authorship includes: "If Paul didn't write the letter, who did? The most plausible suggestion is that Hebrews was actually a sermon Paul gave and it was transcribed later by Luke, a person who would have had the command of the Greek language which the writer shows... There is still much evidence that Paul wrote the letter. The most compelling comes from Scripture itself. Remember that Peter wrote to the Hebrews (that is, the Jews; see Galatians 2:7, 9 and First Peter 1:1). Peter also noted: "...just as our dear brother Paul also wrote you with the wisdom that God gave him" (Second Peter 3:15). In that last verse, Peter is confirming that Paul had also written a letter to the Hebrews!"

Assuming the authorship of Hebrews is Paul, Hebrews 13:18-19 contains this appeal:
- Pray for us.
- We are sure that we have a clear conscience.
- We desire to act honorably in all things.
- Pray for us more earnestly so that I can be restored to you sooner.

John Gills Commentary states:

A clear conscience is a good conscience that is sanctified by the Spirit of God, and sprinkled by the blood of Jesus Christ; here it chiefly respects the upright discharge of it in the ministerial work...

John Gill continues:

In all things willing to live honestly/honorably: not only as men, but as ministers; faithfully dispensing the word of truth, without any regard to the favor or frowns of men, as good stewards of the mysteries of God...

In what area is one to declare honor and prove it by living honorably? In the United States, there has been an ongoing debate and comments made about immigrants and whether or not they are entering the borders of the nation illegally. Is there a right way for one to enter the country? Yes! Are there laws that govern what should be required of anyone seeking asylum? Yes! Are those laws being upheld and enacted? No!

When one seeks to enter this nation legally and become a citizen of the United States, there are some basic requirements. The final one is to take the Naturalization Oath of Allegiance to the United States of America. It is a solemn oath and the applicant for citizenship must repeat:

I hereby declare, on oath, that I absolutely and entirely renounce and abjure all allegiance and fidelity to any foreign prince, potentate, state, or sovereignty, of whom or which I have heretofore been a subject or citizen; that I will support and defend the Constitution and laws of the United States of America against all enemies, foreign and domestic; that I will bear true faith and allegiance to the same; that I will bear arms on behalf of the United States when required by the law; that I will perform noncombatant service in the Armed Forces of the United States when required by the law; that I will perform work of national importance under civilian direction when required by the law; and that I take this obligation freely, without any mental reservation or purpose of evasion; so help me God.

In addition to a formal welcome into the citizenry of the nation, each one who has affirmed the oath is given an American flag. It is held proudly by the recipient.

We tend to forget how the nation was founded. Men of principle wanted to establish a nation that was free of British or any foreign control. To that end, the Fifty-Six men who signed the Declaration of Independence were in agreement as they pledged their lives, their fortunes and their sacred honor. They paid a severe price for having done so. Five signers were captured by the British as traitors and tortured before they died. Twelve had their homes ransacked and burned. Two lost their sons serving in the Revolutionary Army, another had two sons captured. Nine of the Fifty-Six fought and died from wounds or hardships of the Revolutionary War. All of them lost their homes, businesses and possessions. They were treated harshly and some were tortured.

It reminds one of a summary statement about people of faith in Hebrews 11:35-39 which indicates that they lived nobly, honorably and sacrificially. Note how these people of faith are summarized and remembered:

Others were tortured and refused their release, so that they might gain a better resurrection. Still others endured mocking and flogging, and even chains and imprisonment. They were stoned, they were sawed in two, they were put to death by the sword. They went around in sheepskins and goatskins, destitute, oppressed, and mistreated. The world was not worthy of them. They wandered in deserts and mountains, and hid in caves and holes in the ground.

Is this what Paul had in mind when he solicited: "Pray for us, for we are sure that we have a clear conscience, desiring to act honorably in all things"? Yes!

The first military oath under the Constitution was approved by Act of Congress 29 September 1789. It required affirmation to the following:

I, _____ do solemnly affirm to bear true allegiance to the United States of America, and to serve them honestly and faithfully, against all their enemies or opposers whatsoever, and to observe and obey the orders of the President of the United States of America, and the orders of the officers appointed over me.

The next section of that chapter specified that:
the said troops shall be governed by the rules and articles of war, which have been established by the United States in Congress assembled, or by such rules and articles of war as may hereafter by law be established.

Interestingly, the 1789 enlistment oath wasn't changed until 1960 by amendment to Title 10, with the current wording becoming effective in 1962.

In terms of honor and being honorable, the Boy Scout Oath requires the scout to affirm:
On my honor, I will do my best to do my duty to God and my country and to obey the Scout Law; to help other people at all times; to keep myself physically strong, mentally awake and morally straight.

There is also a set of laws that motivate a scout to be: Trustworthy, Loyal, Helpful, Friendly, Courteous, Kind, Obedient, Cheerful, Thrifty, Brave, Clean and Reverent. It all lends itself to the Boy Scout Motto: Always Prepared.

There are several Scripture passages about honor and one's doing what is honorable in God's sight. First would be God's commandment, Exodus 20:12, "Honor your father and your mother, so that you may live long in the land the Lord your God is giving you." These words are repeated by Jesus Christ in Matthew19:19. In First Thessalonians 5:12 (NLT), Paul reminds the church: "Dear brothers and sisters, honor those who are your leaders in the Lord's work. They work hard among you and give you spiritual guidance." For those who are facing hardship, suffering, oppression and persecution, First Peter 2:16-17, "Live as free people, but do not use your freedom as a cover-up for evil; live as God's slaves. Show proper respect to everyone, love the family of believers, fear God, honor the emperor."

Verse 17 (MSG), "Revere God. Respect the government." Verse 17 (AMP), "Show respect for all people [treat them honorably], love the brotherhood (of believers), fear God, honor the king."

A passage that may be difficult to fully understand is

Romans 13:1-7 (MSG). God's Word is inspired and is written for our instruction and godly living. With this in mind, we must remember and do that which Paul has written:

Be a good citizen. All governments are under God. Insofar as there is peace and order, it's God's order. So live responsibly as a citizen. If you're irresponsible to the state, then you're irresponsible with God, and God will hold you responsible. Duly constituted authorities are only a threat if you're trying to get by with something. Decent citizens should have nothing to fear. Do you want to be on good terms with the government? Be a responsible citizen and you'll get on just fine, the government working to your advantage. But if you're breaking the rules right and left, watch out. The police aren't there just to be admired in their uniforms. God also has an interest in keeping order, and He uses them to do it. That's why you must live responsibly—not just to avoid punishment but also because it's the right way to live. That's also why you pay taxes—so that an orderly way of life can be maintained. Fulfill your obligations as a citizen. Pay your taxes, pay your bills, respect your leaders.

In the benediction that closes the book of Hebrews, Paul prays that the Biblical Christian know the reality of God's inner work to: "...equip you with everything good that you may do His will, working in us that which is pleasing in His sight" (Hebrews 13:20).

In 1915, Arthur C. Ainger wrote the words:
> God of our fathers, unto Thee
> Our fathers cried in danger's hour,
> And then Thou gavest them to see
> The acts of Thine almighty power.
> They cried to Thee, and Thou didst hear;
> They called on Thee, and Thou didst save;
> And we their sons today draw near
> Thy name to praise, Thy help to crave.

23. Let Us Honor God

To honor is to: "have and hold in high respect; acknowledging one's worth, merit or rank." A synonym study indicates that honor, honesty, integrity, sincerity refer to the highest moral principles and the absence of deceit or fraud. Honor denotes a fine sense of, and a strict conformity to, what is considered morally right or due. Honesty denotes the presence of probity and particularly the absence of deceit or fraud, especially in business dealings: uncompromising honesty and trustworthiness. Integrity indicates a soundness of moral principle that no power or influence can impair: a man of unquestioned integrity and dependability. Sincerity implies absence of dissimulation or deceit, and a strong adherence to truth. Honor, consideration, distinction refer to the regard in which one is held by others. Honor suggests a combination of liking and respect. Consideration suggests honor because of proven worth. Distinction suggests particular honor because of qualities or accomplishments. The Westminster Shorter Catechism begins with: "Man's chief end is to glorify God and enjoy Him forever." How does one begin to glorify God and enjoy Him? It is part of how one worships the Living God. J.S.B. Monsell captured the idea of worship when he wrote:

O worship the Lord in the beauty of holiness, bow down before Him, His glory proclaim; with gold of obedience and incense of lowliness, kneel and adore Him the Lord is His name.

Fear not to enter His courts in the slenderness of the poor wealth you would count as your own; truth in its beauty and love in its tenderness these are the offerings to bring to His throne.

There are guidelines for one's coming to worship God. What is it that He desires and requires? Psalms 29:1-2, "Ascribe to the Lord, you heavenly beings, ascribe to the Lord glory and strength. Ascribe to the Lord the glory due His name; worship the Lord in the splendor of His holiness." LET US – LET ME remember to honor our God in this way every day. Psalms 96:7-10 goes on to add: "Ascribe to the Lord, all you families of nations, ascribe to the Lord glory and strength. Ascribe to the Lord the glory due His name; bring an offering and come into His courts. Worship the Lord in the splendor of His holiness; tremble before Him, all the earth. Say among the nations, The Lord reigns." LET US – LET ME be committed to bringing Him offerings to be focused on His holiness. May I have the sense (sensation) of the prophet Isaiah when he had the vision of being in the presence of the Living God. His exclamation was: "Woe is me! I am undone! I am a man of unclean lips! I live in a generation of those with unclean thoughts and words"(Isaiah 6:1-9).

What kind of offering can I bring to my God that will please and honor Him? Hebrews 12:15 indicates: "Through Him then LET US continually offer up a sacrifice of praise to God, that is, the fruit of lips that acknowledge His name." What does this mean in one's personal commitment to the Lord? The Pulpit Commentary indicates that it is "the designation in the ritual of the Law of the voluntary peace offering, offered by individuals on occasions calling for special thanksgiving (Leviticus 7:12)…There is a further sacrifice of our own, whereby we must show that we are true partakers of Christ, and truly thankful." It is not what is physically brought to the Lord but the inner and external verbalization of gratitude to the all-sufficient Lord and Savior, Jesus Christ.

First Peter 2:4-5, 9 also expresses this principle of the sacrifice of praise to God:

As you come to Him, the living Stone, rejected by humans but chosen by God and precious to Him, you also, like living stones, are being built into a spiritual house to be a holy priesthood, offering spiritual sacrifices acceptable to God through Jesus Christ.

Peter emphasizes this point in verse 9 when he asserts: "You are a chosen people, a royal priesthood, a holy nation, God's special possession, that you may declare the praises of Him who called you out of darkness into His wonderful light."

In honoring God, it must always be within the context of who He is and in whose presence one has entered. Hebrews 12:28-29 specifies, "Since we are receiving a kingdom that cannot be shaken, LET US be thankful, and so worship God acceptably with reverence and awe, for our God is a consuming fire." Our personal commitment to worship acceptably should always be in terms of reverence and awe.

It reminds one of the old Hymn written by Charles Gabriel (1905), "I stand amazed in the presence Of Jesus the Nazarene, And wonder how He could love me, A sinner, condemned, unclean." One's mind and emotions should always be in terms of whose presence we are in as we purpose to honor the Lord. It is underscored by God's Law, Exodus 20:5 (NLT), "You must not bow down to them (idols, graven images) or worship them, for I, the LORD your God, am a jealous God who will not tolerate your affection for any other gods."

The Lord issues His warning about idolatry in Deuteronomy 4:15-20 (NLT),

But be very careful! You did not see the Lord's form on the day He spoke to you from the heart of the fire at Mount Sinai. So do not corrupt yourselves by making an idol in any form—whether of a man or a woman, an animal on the ground, a bird in the sky, a small animal that scurries along the ground, or a fish in the deepest sea. And when you look up into the sky and see the sun, moon, and stars - all the forces of heaven -don't be seduced into worshiping them. The Lord your God gave them to all the peoples of the earth. Remember that the Lord rescued you from the iron-smelting furnace of Egypt in order to make you His very own people and His special possession, which is what you are today.

Why should this be remembered as one seeks to honor the Living God? Deuteronomy 4:24 (NLT) clearly states the reason: "The Lord your God is a devouring fire; He is a jealous God." The reason and clarification:
- The Lord your God is a devouring fire, and
- He is a jealous God ("My glory I will not give to another." Isaiah 48:11).

The need to honor God aright is shared in Psalm 50:22-23, "Consider this, you who forget God, or I will tear you to pieces, with no one to rescue you: Those who sacrifice thank offerings honor me, and to the blameless I will show my salvation."

All glory, laud and honor,
To Thee, Redeemer, King,
Thou art the king…
The King and Blessed One.

24. Let Us Be Affectionate

For whom do we have and show our greatest affection? What receives most of our time and attention? Do we maintain a serious and devoted relationship to Jesus Christ or to some earthly people or things? Does my insecurities or jealousy affect how I think and act toward others? What about with those who are closest to me, do I genuinely have a deep-rooted affection for them?

I was really moved by a devotional I read that dealt with the writer's struggle with jealousy (C.S., August 2019). He wrote:

For more years than I care to remember, I was consumed with jealousy. I was so insecure and fearful it wasn't uncommon for me to drill my wife with questions - petty, probing questions that were little more than veiled accusations. It is amazing she endured it. Finally, we had one of those famous showdown confrontations every married couple has had. No need to repeat it, but she made it painfully clear that I was smothering her; I was imagining things she never even thought of doing…and it had to stop. Her words hurt, but she did the right thing. I took her seriously.

Jealousy and distrust are at the core of what one should guard against as a follower of Jesus Christ. The previous chapter noted that in the most perfect sense, God is a jealous God and will not share His glory with another. It should not be a surprise that one of the disruptive tools utilized by the enemy of one's soul is the probing of the soul regarding jealousy and trust. The enemy wants to be in control and govern one's thinking and relationships. It is one of those things that is part of the corrupting darkness.

In this regard, Paul directs one's attention to his thoughts in Romans 13:12-14 (NIV), "The night is nearly over; the day is almost here. So LET US put aside the deeds of darkness and put on the armor of light…" An observation that was shared is:

When mankind exists in a state of darkness (sin), he cannot know the Spirit of Truth and Love which comes from God. In a state of darkness, we can so easily fall prey to false teachings and false pathways of life which lead to a state of being lost.

Living in darkness not only affects one's seeing, it also has an impact on what can and will hear. It is helpful to note a statement about the mercies of God in this regard shared in Isaiah 30:20-21,

The Lord will give you the bread of adversity and the water of affliction. Your Teacher will no longer hide Himself, with your own eyes you will see Him. And whether you turn to the right or to the left, your ears will hear His command behind you: This is the way. Walk in it.

The Teacher is the source of the true light. Following Him will prevent one's detours in the ditches of the enemy.

One would do well to remember the mindset of Moses regarding sin and follow his response to it. Hebrews 11:24-26 (ESV) expresses that a choice was made by Moses. He could choose the pleasures and treasures of Egypt or he could choose to reject them even though it would cause suffering and deprivations upon the people of God. His decision:

By faith Moses, when he was grown, refused to be called the son of Pharaoh's daughter. He chose to suffer oppression with God's people rather than the fleeting enjoyment of sin. He valued disgrace for Christ above the treasures of Egypt.

Let Us - Let Me (Seek: Spiritual Maturity)

This is not always an easy choice. It all depends on whether one is stalled at the elementary level of development or has been promoted or graduated to the spiritual growth and knowledge level.

Paul continues his instruction in Romans 13:12-14 by urging: "LET US behave decently, as in the daytime, not in carousing and drunkenness, not in sexual immorality and debauchery, not in dissension and jealousy. Rather, clothe yourselves with the Lord Jesus Christ, and do not think about how to gratify the desires of the flesh." One has to make a decision on wearing the old spiritual wardrobe versus the new. The wise will put away the wardrobe of darkness. With these instructions, LET US return to the devotional mentioned earlier in the chapter: What did the writer do to remedy his inner struggles with jealousy and lack of trust? What did he do about his suspicious thoughts regarding his wife's fidelity? Could he gain victory over this darkness in his heart, soul and mind? Is there a bright light at the end of the dark tunnel for him? Will he hear and heed the words: "This is the way. Walk in it."

He concluded his transparent devotional thoughts by sharing:

I went to work on this ugly side of my life. I confessed my jealousy to my wife. I assured her I would never again treat her with such a lack of trust. I asked God for grace to help, for relief from the destructive habit I had formed, for the ability to love and give myself to this woman without all the choking conditions. I distinctly recall how much an understanding of grace helped. It was as if grace was finally awake in my life, and I could appropriate its power for the first time. It seemed to free me, first in small ways, and finally in major areas. I can honestly say today that I do not entertain a single jealous thought. Grace literally wiped the slate clean.

This is the application of Hebrews 6:1, "LET US move beyond the elementary teachings about Christ and be taken forward to maturity (spiritual growth in the grace and knowledge of the Lord Jesus Christ)." The husband had to find his way out of the web of darkness. He needed to know the affection of Jesus Christ in his life so that he would be affectionate, trusting and edifying in his relationship with his wife. She deserved nothing less. On a personal level, this represented his moving from the elementary level into spiritual maturity.

How then should we be living? What is the hallmark of your life in terms of affection? What is your level of devotion in the affection you have and show? Paul wrote in Romans 12:10 (MSG), "Love from the center of who you are; don't fake it. Run for dear life from evil; hold on for dear life to good. Be good friends who love deeply." The NLT wording is: "Love each other with genuine affection, and take delight in honoring each other."

Peter wrote to the believers of his day, "Summing up: Be agreeable, be sympathetic, be loving, be compassionate, be humble. That goes for all of you, no exceptions. No retaliation. No sharp-tongued sarcasm. Instead, bless - that's your job, to bless. You'll be a blessing and also get a blessing" (First Peter 3:8-9).

The words of Jesus in John 13: 34-35 (MSG) are direct. "Let me give you a new command: Love one another. In the same way I loved you, you love (have affection) one another. This is how everyone will recognize that you are my disciples - when they see the love (the deep affection) you have for each other." A commentator stated: "Your love for each other shall be so decisive evidence that you are like the Savior, that all people shall see and know it. It shall be the thing by which you shall be known among all men. You shall not be known by special rites or habits; not by a special form of dress or manner of speech; not by special austerities and unusual customs, like the Pharisees, the Essenes, or the scribes, but by deep, genuine, and tender affection."

How are you known in your community? When you are away from the church building and church people, what do others observe about you? What would you want it to be? When I was a boy, the church I attended had a ritual that was observed whenever there was a Communion Service. Church members were urged to memorize Romans 12 and First Corinthians 13 so they could be recited at the Communion Service. Back then, Scripture meant King James Version. There was one phrase that fascinated me whenever it was recited. The words in Romans 12:9 (KJV), "Let love be without dissimulation." I don't recall anyone ever explaining that phrase even though everyone dutifully recited it. What does dissimulation mean? "Concealment of the truth about a personal situation; Hypocrisy; Feigning; (to represent fictitiously; put on an appearance of)."

We should clearly and definitively model the words expressed in the Hymn:

> My Jesus, I love Thee,
> I know Thou art mine;
> For Thee all the follies
> of sin I resign.
> My gracious Redeemer,
> my Savior art Thou;
> If ever I loved Thee,
> my Jesus, 'tis now.

25. Let Us Be Compliant

Learning to march in formation is among the many things a military recruit is expected to be compliant with and learn. A role of the drill sergeant is to make certain that the men under his authority learn to keep in step with one another. An old television program, Gomer Pyle - USMC begins with the drill instructor, Vince Carter, shouting out his orders, especially to Gomer, to march in step with the other Marines. Gomer Pyle is jovial, affable and to the best of his ability, responsive. Gomer is known for his innocent simplicity. Sergeant Carter is the opposite. He uses the word "knucklehead" frequently with Gomer. He is loud, demanding and impatient. In one episode, Sergeant Carter tells Gomer that his grandmother once told him that a person ought to do the first thing he was told. It was his way to get the platoon commands taken more seriously by Gomer. The response given by Gomer to Sergeant Carter was: "Well bless her heart." A general theme of the program is the naivete of Gomer and the impatience of Sergeant Carter. The program was never intended to demonstrate Gomer's eventual compliance and ability to march in step with others. It did show that Gomer would gleefully bumble through the drills as best he could.

Is this similar to the way many professing Christians bumble their way through their "Christian" life and relationships within the corps of other professing Christians? Sadly, there are too many who act more like Gomer Pyle than a good soldier of Jesus Christ. They exist in their matter-of-fact world and rarely exhibit their ability to take a serious God seriously. No matter how often they hear God's orders, they slough them off and never fully comply with Him and His marching orders. They pretend they are doing the best they can but the ordinary observer knows they are falling short of that which is expected. They have ears but lack the ability to hear the voice that says to them: "Whether you turn to the right or to the left, your ears will hear a voice behind you, saying: This is the way; walk in it" (Isaiah 30:21). The MSG phrases it: "Your teacher will be right there, local and on the job, urging you on whenever you wander left or right: This is the right road. Walk down this road."

Have you heard that voice of your Teacher? Is your ear attuned to hearing your Teacher today? Most have read the words in Galatians 5:16-17, "Walk by the Spirit, and you will not gratify the desires of the flesh. For the desires of the flesh are against the Spirit, and the desires of the Spirit are against the flesh, for these are opposed to each other, to keep you from doing the things you want to do." Have you read these words? Have you applied these words? Have you heard the Spirit speaking these words to you?

These words are followed by a comparison which is a contrast between the works of the flesh versus the fruit of the Spirit. What should the "professing Christian" see and hear? To begin with, Galatians 5:19-21, "The works of the flesh are evident: sexual immorality, impurity, sensuality, idolatry, sorcery, enmity, strife, jealousy, fits of anger, rivalries, dissensions, divisions, envy, drunkenness, orgies, and things like these. I warn you, as I warned you before, that those who do such things will not inherit the kingdom of God." Do you glean the sense of what is on the heart of God for His people? Do you see and hear His words for you? Are any of these things, stated or implied, a part of your life or thinking? If so, what is the immediate action you should take to bring about correction?

The contrast is quickly revealed in Galatians 5:22-24, "The fruit of the Spirit is love, joy, peace, patience, kindness, goodness, faithfulness, gentleness, self-control; against such things there is no law. And those who belong to Christ Jesus have crucified the flesh with its passions and desires." Do you see and hear that which God wants you to be and model? Why is this choice fundamental for all who would follow Jesus Christ? Why must the "professing Christian" become compliant to these directives originating from the throne of Almighty God? If we parse Galatians 5:16 and 5:25-26, we will learn how the follower of Christ can become all of what God wants one to be.

The phrase, "walk by the Spirit" indicates that one is intended to "walk by the enablement of the Spirit." If and when one does, verse 16 goes on to indicate: "you will not gratify the desires of the flesh." When we consider verses 25-26, we find two hortatory subjunctives. With that as his intention, Paul underscored: "If we live by (the enablement of) the Spirit, there are two hortatory subjunctives one must see, hear and heed:

- **Let us** also keep in step with the Spirit.
- **Let us** not become conceited, provoking one another, envying one another.

Let there be no doubt. The Lord expects each of us who name His name to "keep in step with the Holy Spirit." If or when one fails to hear and do this directive, there are very grave possibilities and consequences. First Thessalonians 5:19 says "Do not quench the Spirit." To quench is equated with putting out the Spirit's fire. Similarly, Paul wrote in Ephesians 4:30 "Do not grieve the Spirit." The meaning is clear. Do not live or behave in such a way that you thwart the Spirit from effectiveness in your life.

How can and how does one either quench or grieve the Spirit? We must hear clearly and be sensitive to the response which is: "Let all bitterness and wrath and anger and clamor (a confused noise) and slander be put away from you, along with all malice." Many would protest that either (a) there was good reason for one to be expressive of some of these things, or (b) it's not a problem for me. I just choose to have nothing to do with such people. Ouch! That is a misapplication of keeping in step with the Spirit. Think about it. Why would you think that your anger, or wrath, etc. is acceptable behavior even though it grieves the Spirit of God and quenches the Spirit in one's life?

The behavior of Jesus Christ's follower who is keeping in step with the Holy Spirit includes (Ephesians 4:32): "Being kind to one another, tenderhearted, forgiving one another, as God in Christ forgave you." Does this describe the pattern of your behavior and lifestyle? If not, why not?

We all need to prayerfully consider these things and make certain that our lives are compliant with God's directives for them.

26. Let Us Be A Do-Gooder

How is a child of God supposed to relate towards fellow-believers? What Biblical obligations, if any, does one have toward non-believers? Luke 10:25-29 reveals an answer in a brief dialogue.

On one occasion an expert in the law stood up to test Jesus. Teacher, he asked: What must I do to inherit eternal life? What is written in the Law? Jesus replied. How do you read it? The expert answered: Love the Lord your God with all your heart and with all your soul and with all your strength and with all your mind; and, love your neighbor as yourself. Jesus replied: You have answered correctly: Do this and you will live. But the expert wanted to justify himself, so he asked Jesus: And who is my neighbor?

How will Jesus respond to the expert? Will he accept the feigned indifference of the expert? No! The expert was functioning with tunnel vision (an extremely narrow or prejudiced outlook; narrow-mindedness). Jesus proceeds to share with him, Luke 10:30-37, the parable of the Good Samaritan. The issue on the heart of Jesus was dealing with one's spirit of mercy and compassion. He is interested in how one responds in a time of crisis and need. If one knows the heart of Jesus, he will act accordingly by showing mercy and offering assistance. If one is self-indulgent, he will act with indifference. These are the same concerns Jesus addressed in Matthew 25:31-46 when He was separating the sheep from the goats. His point was there are a lot of people who have needs and are in stressful situations. The Biblical follower of Jesus Christ is diligent and spontaneous in responding to the needs of others around them. They respond instinctively. They don't need any organized appeal or pressure applied. They function in an uninhibited manner and with the sensitivity that but for the grace of God go I.

In Luke 10:30-37, Jesus dramatizes the point he wants to make. He tells a true-to-life story. A traveler is treated inhumanely. He is attacked, beaten and robbed. He is left on the roadside half-dead to fend for himself or die. But the road is travelled by other people. Jesus indicates that a priest was going down the same road, he saw the man and his condition, but decided to having nothing to do with him. He crossed the road and by-passed the man in need. Later on, another religious person, a Levite, came to the place where the injured man was laying. He saw him but chose to cross the road and pass by on the other side. Two religious people saw the man with a need but rationalized and decided that they had neither the time nor resources to help him. A missed opportunity of exhibiting Biblical love? Yes! A denial of any role of showing mercy and compassion toward a needy person? Yes!

In verses 33 through 35,

A Samaritan, as he traveled, came where the man was; and when he saw him, he took pity on him. He went to him and bandaged his wounds, pouring on oil and wine. Then he put the man on his own donkey, brought him to an inn and took care of him. The next day he took out two denarii (a denarius was the usual daily wage of a day laborer) and gave them to the innkeeper. Look after him, he said, and when I return, I will reimburse you for any extra expense you may have.

The Samaritan had a place to go but he made time to look after a wounded and dying stranger. He stayed with him and nursed him as best as he could. He was gracious and generous to the stranger and made provision for his needs to be met. He indicated to the inn-keeper to look after him and if there were additional expenses, he would care for them when he returned. The Samaritan became engaged with a stranger, his need and health.

This brought Jesus to a question directed to the expert in the Law, verses 36-37: "Which of these three do you think was a neighbor to the man who fell into the hands of robbers?" Without hesitancy, the expert in the Law responded with the obvious and correct answer: "The one who had mercy on him." This is the correct answer but there can be miles of difference between giving the right answer versus doing the right thing in one's caring about and for others. Jesus's command to the expert in the law is also His command to us: "Go and do likewise." There can be no evasion of the directive stated by Jesus. The language He used was basic and understandable: "Go" and "Do,"

Paul made an obvious connection and application of the words of Jesus when he wrote in Galatians 6:9-10, "Let us not become weary in doing good, for at the proper time we will reap a harvest if we do not give up. Therefore, as we have opportunity, let us do good to all people, especially to those who belong to the family of believers." The special emphasis is in the two directives that need to be enacted at all times:

- Let Us not become weary in doing good…
- Let Us do good to all people, especially to those who belong to the family of believers…

A truth that Paul wanted his readers to note was that the Christian life was never intended to be self-indulgent but to always be sensitive to other people with whom one has contact. When one is sensitive to the life and need of others, one will react: "as we have opportunity." His point is that there are all kinds of opportunities and challenges. We need to be aware of them and ready to do what we can for whoever we can. The opportunity should always receive a positive response. Paul follows up on that phrase by adding: "Let Us not become weary in doing good…Let us do good to all people, especially to those who belong to the family of God." Implied in these words is the fact that there will always be needs to which one can respond. There will always be opportunities that require one's attention. Paul is also saying that at times it may all seem to be insurmountable but one must not let weariness interfere with one's doing good in behalf of others. Always be cheerful and never complaining when engaged in the opportunities God is entrusting to you.

> I'm so glad I'm a part of the family of God;
> I've been washed in the fountain,
> cleansed by His blood!
> Joint heirs with Jesus as we travel this sod,
> For I'm part of the family,
> the family of God.

27. Let Us Be Non-Discriminatory

In a day when political correctness has dominated cultural interaction and communication, it has become a concern of what one can do or say lest some other person or group is offended by one's speech or action. Freedom of speech is almost relegated to antiquity unless the "speech-police" wish to use it to their advantage. Who one chooses to talk to and what was said during a conversation is scrutinized and often criticized. In John 4, "political correctness" was part of the question raised when Jesus visited with a woman at the well. Jesus and His disciples have left Judea and were heading back to Galilee. The journey took them through Samaria and they stopped for a rest at Sychar. The disciples left Jesus to go into town to buy food. While they were away, Jesus was sitting by Jacob's well. A Samaritan woman came to get water and approached the well at noon. Jesus asked her: "Will you give me a drink?"

It is obvious that she doesn't know who has asked for a drink. Her conclusion was that He was a Jewish man. It is at this point that an ageless discriminatory issue was raised by the woman. John 4:9 is a critical passage in this regard. She responded to Jesus: "You are a Jew and I am a Samaritan woman. How can you ask me for a drink?" (For Jews do not associate with Samaritans.) The MSG phrases the verse: "The Samaritan woman, taken aback, asked: How come you, a Jew, are asking me, a Samaritan woman, for a drink?" (Jews in those days wouldn't be caught dead talking to Samaritans.) The NLT paraphrases the verse: "The woman was surprised, for Jews refuse to have anything to do with Samaritans. She said to Jesus: You are a Jew, and I am a Samaritan woman. Why are you asking me for a drink?" At that point there was a sharp shift in the conversation (Verses 10-15). Jesus raised four major points.

The first major point was His reference to living water that He alone can give to her. The woman stated the obvious that He didn't have a bucket to get any water to satisfy His own thirst. How could He possibly fulfill the statement that He will give her living water. He explained to her the difference between well-water versus the spring of water welling up to eternal life. The result was that Jesus whet her curiosity and desire to have access to such water. In verse 15, she said to Jesus: "Sir, give me this water that I won't get thirsty and have to keep coming here to draw water."

The second major point Jesus raised with her was the sanctity and fidelity associated with marriage. Jesus said to her: "Go, call your husband and come back." Without any hesitancy, she replied: "I have no husband." Jesus disclosed more about Himself when He said to her (verses 17-18): "You are right when you say you have no husband. The fact is, you have had five husbands, and the man you now have is not your husband. What you have just said is quite true."

The third major issue is raised by the woman. In her attempt to change the discussion, she raised her thoughts about worship (verses 19-26). She concluded that He is a prophet. She then asserts that she is part of a religious group that has worshipped on the mountain that was before them. She contrasted this with her declaration (verse 20): "You Jews claim that the place where we must worship is in Jerusalem." Jesus then clarified what true worship is for anyone who enters into the salvation available through the Jews. Jesus said (verses 22-24): "You Samaritans worship what you do not know; we worship what we do know, for salvation is from the Jews. Yet a time is coming and has now come when the true worshipers will worship the Father in the Spirit and in truth, for they are the kind of worshipers the Father seeks. God is spirit, and his worshipers must worship in the spirit and in truth." The woman wistfully said to Jesus (verse 25-26): "I know that Messiah is coming. When He comes, He will explain everything to us." Jesus clarified that which she had just asserted when He declared; I, the one speaking to you, I am He."

The fourth major issue that Jesus raised pertained to evangelism and outreach. The disciples returned from their grocery shopping trip and saw Jesus speaking with a woman. They don't say anything about it. Instead, the disciples urged Jesus to eat some of the food they had purchased. Jesus told them (verse 32): "I have food to eat that you know nothing about." The disciples have no idea what He was speaking about. Jesus emphasized (verse 35): "Don't you have a saying: It's still four months until harvest'? I tell you, open your eyes and look at the fields! They are ripe for harvest." Be alert! Be ready to tell all people that Jesus is the Messiah (the Christ). The disciples are about to learn an important lesson about evangelism.

What did Jesus want His disciples to see? What were they supposed to be looking at? Their answer is found in verses 39-42. It would seem as though Jesus pointed in the direction of the town of Sychar. The woman gave her testimony about meeting Jesus and all that He had told her. As a result, many of the people believed Jesus was the Messiah. The Samaritans came to Him (verses 40-42) and they urged Him to stay with them. Jesus stayed for two days. "Because of His words many more became believers." The Samaritans testified (verse 42): "We no longer believe just because of what you said; now we have heard for ourselves, and we know that this man really is the Savior of the world."

Both the professing Christian and Biblical Christian have a similarity when it comes to outreach and evangelism. Neither group would readily admit that they discriminate. However, barriers are established regarding who will be invited to attend "our church" and who will be evangelized. Peter had a problem in this regard. Paul came and confronted him about his duplicity and discrimination. Galatians 2:1-21 is one of the key passages where Paul confronts Peter publicly about his hypocrisy. Peter was publically condemning what he himself practiced privately because of the fear of criticism. Peter was neither bound by law nor the traditions being promoted by the Judaizers, but by his separation from the Gentiles he was supporting the idea that the Gentiles should be a separate "denomination". Peter had been eating meals with these Christians on a regular basis. A Jew sharing meals with a Gentile was something that was unacceptable according to Jewish tradition (Acts 10:28). However, God nullified this tradition when He told Peter in a vision that Gentiles should not be considered unclean (Acts 10:1-11:18). This acceptance of Gentile Christians was later reaffirmed during the Jerusalem Council (Acts 15:1-29).

The problem arose when some Jews from Jerusalem arrived in Antioch. Peter gradually withdrew from eating with the Gentile Christians, and instead ate with the Jewish Christians. Galatians 2:12 indicates he did this because he feared these Jews. He likely "feared" them because he wanted to be liked and popular, plus he probably did not want word to get back to Jerusalem that he was eating with the Gentiles. Peter's primary sin (as well as the other Jews who followed his lead) was that he "walked not uprightly according to the truth of the gospel" (Galatians 2:14). Because of this action, Paul called Peter a hypocrite. Peter believed one thing, but did something else. As a leader in the church, he was to set a good example for others, but instead, his hypocritical actions led others astray.

If we fast forward to the 21st century church, do we find hypocrisy in our outreach effort and fellowship with those of like precious faith? In too many situations, the answer is a resounding, Yes! If only the powerful song sung by Sandi

Patty would become the reality in the general ministry of the missional church.

> Love in any language.
> Straight from the heart;
> Brings us all-together; Never apart...
> Love in any language,

28. Let Us Be Appreciative

The idea of gratitude, appreciation and thankfulness is stated throughout the Bible. It is succinctly stated: "Give thanks in all circumstances; for this is the will of God in Christ Jesus for you" (First Thessalonians 5:18). This should be a sufficient basis for showing appreciation and giving thanks for events and blessings that are part of one's experiences. One of the inferred "let us" obligations pertains to ministry and ministers and the appreciation one has for the faithfulness that is modeled. This is also stated succinctly: "Remember your leaders, those who spoke to you the word of God. Consider the outcome of their way of life, and imitate their faith" (Hebrews 13:7).

There is a spiritual issue at the core of one's life if there is no understanding or demonstration of a thankful spirit. My opinion is that anyone who is in a church leadership position should give evidence of a thankful heart and spirit. They should have the Psalmist's words saturating their minds and hearts: "Enter His gates with thanksgiving, and His courts with praise! Give thanks to Him; bless His name! For the Lord is good; His steadfast love endures forever, and His faithfulness to all generations" (Psalms 100:4-5). They should also be committed to and expected to live as they: "Serve the Lord with gladness!" (Psalms 100:1).

There should also be an understanding and adherence to the words spoken by Jesus Christ. The word blessed has some vital qualities:

- Blessed [spiritually prosperous, to be admired] are the poor in spirit
- Blessed [forgiven, refreshed by God's grace] are those who mourn [over their sins which leads to repentance]

- Blessed [inwardly peaceful, spiritually secure, worthy of respect] are the gentle[the kind-hearted, the sweet-spirited, the self-controlled], for they will inherit the earth.
- Blessed [joyful, nourished by God's goodness] are those who hunger and thirst for righteousness [those who actively seek right standing with God]
- Blessed [content, sheltered by God's promises] are the merciful
- Blessed [anticipating God's presence, spiritually mature] are the pure in heart[those with integrity, moral courage, and godly character]
- Blessed [spiritually calm with life-joy in God's favor] are the makers *and* maintainers of peace, for they will express His character
- Blessed [comforted by inner peace and God's love] are those who are persecuted
- Blessed [morally courageous and spiritually alive with life-joy in God's goodness] are you when people insult you and persecute you, and falsely say all kinds of evil things against you (Matthew 5:3-11 AMP).

In case one cannot think of things for which thanks can and should be given, August L. Storm (1891) penned the words of a hymn for the Swedish Salvation Army that expresses some reasons why the child of God should be thankful:

Thanks to God for my Redeemer,
Thanks for all Thou dost provide!
Thanks for times now but a memory,
Thanks for Jesus by my side!
Thanks for pleasant, balmy springtime,
Thanks for dark and stormy fall!
Thanks for tears by now forgotten,
Thanks for peace within my soul!

> Thanks for prayers that Thou hast answered,
> Thanks for what Thou dost deny!
> Thanks for storms that I have weathered,
> Thanks for all Thou dost supply!
> Thanks for pain, and thanks for pleasure,
> Thanks for comfort in despair!
> Thanks for grace that none can measure,
> Thanks for love beyond compare!
>
> Thanks for roses by the wayside,
> Thanks for thorns their stems contain!
> Thanks for home and thanks for fireside,
> Thanks for hope, that sweet refrain!
> Thanks for joy and thanks for sorrow,
> Thanks for heavenly peace with Thee!
> Thanks for hope in the tomorrow,
> Thanks through all eternity!

Over the years, I have attempted to be consistent in sharing with friends and associates that I appreciate them. I never know how those words are received. I only know that when they are communicated they are sincere. Should there be one with whom I have disagreement, I try to find something about them so, that like Paul, I can write, "I thank God for my remembrance of you." To be very transparent, I have done this as best as I can (and with the Lord's help) to disallow any bitterness or retaliation creeping into my thought-life about other people or organizations.

It is disconcerting to observe those who claim to be following Jesus Christ's model who vocalize that they are the ones calling the shots and making the decisions. If I could, I would try to remedy that viewpoint. However, my effort would be a very poor substitute for the Holy Spirit's convicting and convincing (John 16:7-11).

Several years ago, The Promise Keepers wrote a prayer chorus that should be sung by each of us as often as possible. I can only hope that the desire of my heart and yours will echo this prayer:

> Purify my heart,
> Let me be as gold and precious silver.
> Purify my heart,
> Let me be as gold, pure gold.
> (Chorus)
> Refiner's fire,
> My heart's one desire
> Is to be... holy;
> Set apart for You, Lord.
> I choose to be... holy;
> Set apart for You, my Master,
> Ready to do Your will.
>
> Purify my heart,
> Cleanse me from within
> And make me holy.
> Purify my heart,
> Cleanse me from my sin,
> deep within.

29. Let Us Be Light And Salt

In His Sermon on the Mount, Jesus taught His disciples two significant truths about becoming and being the salt of the earth and the light of the world. When one thinks about it, some of the disciples who had been fishermen may have used "salty" (racy or course) language as they set sail and fished. Jesus was telling them that their language was to be used differently if they followed Him. They were to speak in such a way that it would have a positive and lasting result in the lives of those with whom they would have contact. When Jesus referenced being light, He was aware that the fishermen did much of their fishing during the night. However, their lives were to now radiate the light of the world, Jesus Christ, in all they did, wherever they went and in what they said, both day and night. This was what Jesus taught, expressed and emphasized with His disciples:

You are the salt of the earth. But if the salt loses its saltiness, how can it be made salty again? It is no longer good for anything, except to be thrown out and trampled underfoot. You are the light of the world. A town built on a hill cannot be hidden. Neither do people light a lamp and put it under a bowl. Instead they put it on its stand, and it gives light to everyone in the house. In the same way, let your light shine before others, that they may see your good deeds and glorify your Father in heaven" (Matthew 5:13-16).

There is an adage that says: "Seeing is believing." Jesus underscored this truth with His disciples when He established what they were to be and how they were to impact their world for Him. One of the truths and basic principles they would have to learn was later expressed in First John 4:7. "Beloved, LET US love one another, for love is from God, and whoever loves has been born of God and knows God." John is echoing that which Jesus Christ instructed: "This is my command: Love each other" (John 15:17). Jesus expressed this dynamic earlier when He taught: "A new commandment I give to you, that you love one another; as I have loved you, that you also love one another. By this all will know that you are My disciples, if you have love for one another" (John 13:34-35 NKJV).

In a book written by Gene Edwards, *A Tale Of Three Kings* (A Study In Brokenness), the author shares his insights about the first three kings of Israel. King Saul who was wanted by the people; King David who was wanted by God; and Absalom who wanted the throne and forcefully made himself king in place of his father David. The key to the narrative is how David responded to Saul and how he would react to Absalom. When David was being advised by Nathan the prophet, Zadok the priest and Abishai on how he should respond to his son's disrespect and opposition, the author's narrative indicates the heart of David and His love for God and His will for David and the kingdom:

It is better that I be defeated, even killed, than to learn the ways of a Saul or the ways of an Absalom. The kingdom is not that valuable. Let him have it, if that be the Lord's will. I repeat: I shall not learn the ways of either Saul or Absalom... I did not lift a finger to be made king. Nor shall I do so to preserve a kingdom. Even the kingdom of God! God put me here. It is not my responsibility to take, or keep, authority. Do you not realize, it may be His will for these things to take place? If He chooses, God can protect and keep the kingdom even now. After all, it is His kingdom...

No man knows. Only God knows, and He has not spoken. I did not fight to be king, and I will not fight to remain king. May God come tonight and take the throne, the kingship, and...His anointing from me. I seek His will, not His power. I repeat, I desire His will more than I desire a position of leadership. He may be through with me...

Abishai called out once more, softly this time. Admiration flashed across his face: Good King, thank you. For what? the puzzled king asked as he turned back in the doorway. Not for what you have done, but for what you have not done...Thank you for suffering, for being willing to lose everything. Thank you for giving God a free hand to end, and even destroy, your kingdom - if it pleases him. Thank you for being an example to us all.

The words expressed by Abishai about King David being an example summarized David's heart and desire in loving the Lord His God with all of his heart, soul, strength and mind. Abishai was also thankful for David's readiness and willingness for all the will of God to take place in his life and the kingdom. David's personal love for God was far greater than his love for anything else. That love would be expressed by his actions when his suffering was greatest and his future unknown. He was content to keep in step with the leading of the Lord in and for his life. Wherever the Lord took him or whatever the Lord allowed to occur in his life, David was content that he was the Lord's and content in the center of God's will for him.

David's heart was oriented and committed to the words Paul wrote: "LET US not become weary in doing good, for at the proper time we will reap a harvest if we do not give up. Therefore, as we have opportunity, LET US do good to all people, especially to those who belong to the family of believers" (Galatians 6:9-10).

The reality of these words were apparent when King Saul's jealousy and anger were such that he wanted David dead. Several times, Saul had thrown spears at David in the hope that he would kill him – but each effort by Saul failed. The heart of David regarding King Saul was evidenced one day in a cave. David and his men were in the back of the cave when King Saul entered it to take care of his personal needs.

While sitting there, King Saul fell asleep. David's men whispered to him that now was the moment when he could avenge himself against the king. David did crawl up and cut a portion off of Saul's garment. Even that act affected David's conscience because he had disrespected the anointed king. David said to his men: "The Lord forbid that I should do such a thing to my master, the Lord's anointed, or lay my hand on him; for he is the anointed of the Lord" (First Samuel 24:6).

How did the idea from Galatians 6:9-10 of "not being weary in doing good" work out in David's relationship with King Saul? The words of the king gives the answer: "Saul asked: Is that your voice, David my son? And he wept aloud. You are more righteous than I, he said. You have treated me well, but I have treated you badly. You have just now told me about the good you did to me; the Lord delivered me into your hands, but you did not kill me. When a man finds his enemy, does he let him get away unharmed? May the Lord reward you well for the way you treated me today. I know that you will surely be king and that the kingdom of Israel will be established in your hands" (First Samuel 24:16-20). As David was with Saul, you and I should be with all people at all times as we obediently follow Jesus Christ who mandated that we are to be salt and light in this world for Him.

David's journey with the Lord was very similar to one's walk with the Lord today. To be "salt" and "light" in a world that is contrary to Biblical values can easily become wearisome. It is vital that one retain a focus upon God – His will and His holiness. A previously quoted Hymn written by Phillip P. Bliss (1873) is useful as a prayer for one's journey and service for the Lord:

> More holiness give me, more strivings within.
> More patience in suffering, more sorrow for sin.
> More faith in my Savior, more sense of His care.
> More joy in His service, more purpose in prayer.

More gratitude give me…More zeal for His glory, More hope in His Word…More meekness in trial, more praise for relief.

30. Let Us Be Recognizable

The overall objectives of the "LET US" passages throughout the word of God are twofold: (a) that we live a worthy and honorable life before the Lord and watching world; and (b) that we finish well in the race that is before us. Obviously, there are particular criteria that are indispensable for the Biblical Christian.

- The Beatitudes are basic principles by which one's life is to be measured and lived (Matthew 5:3-11)
- To follow Jesus' instruction to be both salt and light in the world – piercing the darkness and making an eternal difference in individual lives (Matthew 5:13-16)
- To seek first the kingdom of God and His righteousness rather than being filled with anxiety and worry (Matthew 6:25-34)
- To rid oneself of the lusts of the flesh and fill oneself with the fruit of the Spirit (Galatians 5:16-17)
- To live in a purposeful way by the enablement of the Holy Spirit and to always keep in step with Him (Galatians 5:25-26)
- To be careful that the Spirit is neither quenched (First Thessalonians 5:19) nor grieved (Ephesians 4:30) by one's careless living
- To live within the guidelines for one's life based upon God's power and promises (First Peter 1:3-4)
- To be a person of unwavering faith and believing that nothing is impossible with God. Knowing that He is able to do immeasurably more than we can ask or think or imagine (Ephesians 3:20)
- To commit one's way (Psalm 37:5) and one's work (Proverbs 16:3) to the Lord

- To practice quietness in the presence of the Lord (Psalm 46:10) and patience as one waits upon Him (Psalm 37:7)
- To learn to be governed by God's peace (John 14:27; 16:33; Psalm 23; Philippians 4:6-7)
- To be a person who does good whenever and wherever one can (Galatians 6:9-10)
- To keep one's focus on Jesus only (Hebrews 12:2)
- To be confident of the Lord's strength available for you (Isaiah 40:31)
- To finish well the tasks the Lord has assigned to you and the journey He has set before you (Hebrews 12:1, Second Timothy 4:7, Philippians 2:16 and 3:12)

This is just a short list of the character traits the Lord requires of His followers. Does He recognize you? Is He honored by your life? Do others see Jesus in your daily life or just at a morning worship service?

Two old quiz shows had a similar format. One was *What's My Line?* The other was *To Tell The Truth*. After three people, two of whom were imposters, were interviewed by and voted upon by a panel of four, the Moderator would say, "Will the real_____, please stand up!" Several times the panel had chosen the wrong person. Abraham Lincoln was quoted as having said: "You can fool some of the people some of the time but you can't fool all of the people all of the time." This statement should be considered as one measures one's life against the various character traits for a Biblical Christian. There will be a day when all stand before the Lord and the "real" follower of Jesus Christ will be fully known. The imposters will be cast off forever.

A worship chorus expresses how one's life and relationship to Jesus Christ must be if one is to be recognizable and finish well.

You are my strength when I am weak
You are the treasure that I seek

Let Us - Let Me (Seek: Spiritual Maturity)

> You are my all in all
> Seeking You as a precious jewel
> Lord, to give up I'd be a fool
> You are my all in all
>
> Taking my sin, my cross, my shame
> Rising again I bless Your name
> You are my all in all
> When I fall down You pick me up
> When I am dry You fill my cup
> You are my all in all
>
> Jesus, Lamb of God
> Worthy is Your name
> Jesus, Lamb of God
> Worthy is Your name.

What should be foremost in one's thinking if the accepted goal is to finish well? What is the context in which we are to live and what is the cause of urgency that we are to never forget? Paul specifies meaningfully when he wrote:

The night is nearly over; the day is almost here. So LET US put aside the deeds of darkness and put on the armor of light. LET US behave decently, as in the daytime, not in carousing and drunkenness, not in sexual immorality and debauchery, not in dissension and jealousy. Rather, clothe yourselves with the Lord Jesus Christ, and do not think about how to gratify the desires of the flesh." Romans 13:12-14 (NIV).

Eugene Peterson used clear and unique words as he paraphrased Scripture. His insights regarding how one can finish well are (MSG):

Don't burn out; keep yourselves fueled and aflame. Be alert servants of the Master, cheerfully expectant. Don't quit in hard times; pray all the harder. Help needy Christians; be inventive in hospitality. Bless your enemies; no cursing under your breath. Laugh with your happy friends when they're happy; share tears when they're down. Get along with each other; don't be stuck-up. Make friends with nobodies; don't be the great somebody (Romans 12:11-16).

A prayer hymn my wife and I requested to be sung at our wedding expressed how we wanted to live throughout all of our days and allow us to finish well. We personalized the words of the Hymn so that they expressed our commitment to each other as well as to the Lord.

>Teach us Thy way, O Lord, Teach us Thy way!
>Thy guiding grace afford, Teach us Thy way!
>Help us to walk aright, More by faith, less by sight;
>Lead us with heavenly light, Teach us Thy way!

>When we are sad at heart, Teach us Thy way!
>When earthly joys depart, Teach us Thy way!
>In hours of loneliness, In times of dire distress,
>In failure or success, Teach us Thy way!

>When doubts and fears arise, Teach us Thy way!
>When storms overspread the skies,
>Teach us Thy way!
>Shine through the cloud and rain,
>Through sorrow, toil and pain;
>Make Thou our pathway plain, Teach us Thy way!

>Long as our lives shall last, Teach us Thy way!
>Wherever our lot be cast, Teach us Thy way!
>Until the race is run, Until the journey's done,
>Until the crown is won, Teach us Thy way!

This was our prayer on our wedding day and it is our continuing prayer for each new day. We want our lives to fit into God's plan. We want to finish well so that He will be the one who receives the glory and praise.

Epilogue

In the early chapters of this book, reference was made to Psalms 95 and the number of "LET US" phrases used by the Psalmist. His emphasis was upon how and why one should enthusiastically worship the Lord Biblically. The Psalmist made a historical reference about the children of Israel but made no reference to formats, rituals or customs required for one's worship of the Lord.

When Jesus walked in the midst of the seven churches (Revelation 1 and 2) and assessed their level of commitment, His concluding words to each church He addressed was: "He who has ears to hear, let him hear what the Spirit is saying to the church." The Psalmist used a similar statement in the overall consideration one gives to worship: "Today, if you hear His voice, do not harden your hearts..." (Psalms 96:7-8 ESV).

One of the encouragements in this book is to have the reader personalize the key phrase. In place of "LET US", one should personalize the phrase to be "LET ME." Why should this be done? Because, the Scriptures principally teach what one is to believe concerning God and the duty God requires of each one. This is why "LET US/LET ME" is not a suggestion but a direction for one to live by. It is a mandate for one's life and ultimate happiness in the Lord.

A hymn was written by Leander L. Pickett (1902) that paraphrases the commission of Jesus Christ and captures the "LET US" of the inspired writers of Scripture: (LET US – LET ME):

> Go and tell the joyful tidings,
> Jesus died to save,
> Rose again in holy triumph,
> Conquering the grave.

> Tell His power to loose the captive,
> Set the prisoner free,
> And proclaim to eager millions
> Glorious Jubilee.

May the Lord enrich your life and grant you His strength for each new day.

May you enthusiastically embrace and attach "LET ME" to your life's commitment to and service for the Lord Jesus Christ.

About the Author

James Perry has served the Church with more than 54 years of continuous ministry. He attended Columbia Bible College (now Columbia International University) for three years; transferring to Covenant College, a new Presbyterian College in St. Louis, MO from which he graduated with a B.A. in Philosophy. After graduation, he enrolled in Covenant Theological Seminary where he received a B.D. in theology, and returned later for his M.A. He and his wife make their home in Centreville, AL; He has four children; 16 Grandchildren and 14 Great Grandchildren. He is the Author of 11 Books (all of which are available on Amazon).

www.ingramcontent.com/pod-product-compliance
Lightning Source LLC
Chambersburg PA
CBHW031643040426
42453CB00006B/196